China

formation and development

whitney

china

formation and development

First published in 1998 by ●●●ellipsis
2 Rufus Street, London N1 6PE

Published in the United States by Whitney Library of Design,
an imprint of Watson-Guptill Publications,
a division of BPI Communications, Inc.
1515 Broadway, New York, New York 10036

ISBN 0-8230-0383-3

Publisher Tom Neville
Designed by Jonathan Moberly
Edited by Vicky Wilson
Drawings by John Hewitt
Drawing on pages 162–163 generated by Matthew Taylor from
a CAD model by Veronica Antoniou, Kent Institute of Art and
Design, Canterbury
Glossary by Andrew Wyllie
Index by Diana LeCore
Printed and bound in Hong Kong

Library of Congress Catalog Card Number: 98-87113

First printing, 1998

1 2 3 4 5 6 7 8 9 / 06 05 04 03 02 01 00 99 98

contents

China's recorded history goes back to the mid-second millennium BC. One of the seminal civilisations of the world was evolving on the banks of east Asia's great rivers – the Huang He, Yangtze and Zhu He – well before that time, but the first of the long line of dynasties that were to mould Chinese history, the Shang, emerged to the north of the Yangtze in the 16th century BC in the wake of the shadowy Xia dynasty. The Shang were hardly yet an imperial dynasty effectively ruling over the territory now thought of as China, but they exercised authority strong enough to organise labour for flood control and irrigation, and were feudal overlords claiming suzerainty over many princes who held small states on fief in return for the provision of tribute and troops. Walled towns, centred on the granaries in which the tribute was stored, were the bases of the rulers. Thus, though agricultural, Chinese society was town-based from the outset and the idea of the walled enclosure was peculiarly predominant in Chinese architectural history.

Doubtless indebted to the Xia, the Shang could write in standardised characters, at first to record ora-

1 **Imperial City** Ming scroll painting.

cles on prepared bone. They were also masters of bronze casting for weapons, armour and ritual objects interred with sustenance in their elaborate graves. Equipped with chariots, horses and armies of sacrificed human retainers, these graves were clearly designed for eternity and with a belief in the eternal existence of soul-prompted ancestor worship to protect the clan and to ensure generation. There was also a primitive animism devoted to the spirits of mountains, rivers and other natural phenomena but, above all, there was the divine force of nature on whose sufferance man was constrained – hence the existence of oracles and the recording of them. This duality in worship was perpetuated throughout Chinese dynastic history in the dedication of twin urban temples to heaven and earth.

The Shang were supplanted by the Zhou dynasty, propelled from the west by better cavalry, who established their capital near modern Xi'an and ruled most of the north from the mid-11th to the beginning of the 8th centuries BC. Their power began to wane in the 8th century, but they staggered on until the 5th century BC. They sustained Shang beliefs, but established the law of primogeniture to stabilise the succession and to bind it to ancestor worship. Shang practices too were sustained, including flood control and water conservation, and water-borne transport was developed. Agriculture expanded in consequence, especially after the introduction of iron led to the mass production of efficient tools.

With the development of manufacturing and trade in the produce of a flourishing countryside, the cities grew in importance and a monetary economy emerged. But with the expansion of agriculture went an extension of the fief system. Central control weakened and after the 8th century BC it was undermined by the constant pressure of nomadic tribes from the north and west. Forced to abandon their western provinces, the Zhou established a new capital at Luoyang (Wangchang), but their supremacy was nominal by the end of the 5th century BC and their vassals asserted independence in several 'Warring States'.

Confucianism and Daoism

Nearly two centuries of turmoil naturally produced diversity, in particular of custom, economy, measurement, money, script and schools of thought. The most important of the last in shaping Chinese civilisation ever after were the complementary philosophies of Confucianism and Daoism. Their teachers, Kong Fuzi (whose name was Latinised by the Jesuits as Confucius) and Laozi (if, in fact, he existed), were born in the last century of the Zhou era, when the political situation was already confused. Striving to cope with the confusion and to restore order, Confucius recalled a Golden Age of orthodox authority.[1] The Daoists, on the other hand, sought escape from society in a mystical union with nature.[2]

Devoted to the study of history and ancient ritual, Confucius (c. 550–479 BC) started a school of government (personal and political) when 22 years old. For 30 years he continued to study and teach in private, attracting many disciples until he was called to public service where he rose to high office, reputedly banishing crime and strengthening the ruler at the expense of his feudatories. Undermined by foreign agents he went into self-imposed exile and wandered from state to state looking for a prince who would accept his guidance for the right ordering of his kingdom. He returned home disappointed when 69 years of age and declined office to perfect his teaching, based largely on history and the rituals at the base of order in antiquity.

Governed by propriety in the Confucian Golden Age, the individual's place in society was recognised as one of subordination to authority – servant to master, woman to man, all to the head of the family and beyond to the head of the state. The supreme authority was the will of heaven (*qi*, analogous to the Shang spirit of nature) manifest on earth, through primogeniture, in the son of heaven – the emperor. And the emperor held the mandate of heaven, to sustain morality and material prosperity, in perpetual harmony with *qi*: out of harmony he lost the mandate as any man out of tune with nature failed in his purpose. Hence the importance of *feng shui*, harmonisation with nature.

Central to the Confucian ideal were the elevation of society through virtue (*de*) and its regulation through ritual (*li*). Virtue, conferred by heaven, and ritual, derived from the ancients, effected government by ethical example and were cultivated by 'the gentleman' in his commitment to morality – not to gain access to heaven but for their own sake on earth. The gentleman, thus, was defined not only by his qualities – benevolence and responsibility, righteousness and respectfulness – but also by the courage and erudition cultivated in sport and study. If the Golden Age set the example, education was the means for its emulation, and examination was the ordeal to be undergone by those fit to serve the ruler, the servant of virtue endowed with the mandate of heaven to regulate the lives of men. The followers of Confucius, then, were conservative, authoritarian and rational: veneration for precedent, excellence and hierarchy perfectly recommended their way as the orthodoxy of bureaucratic imperialism.

Anti-rational and anti-authoritarian, the followers of Laozi were obsessed with the concept of the *dao* – the 'way', the hidden power of nature generated by the interaction of the polar opposites, *yang* and *yin* (male and female, active and passive, etc.). This was inapprehensible, but the individual could comprehend harmony with it through physical and emotional suppleness. That could be developed only through withdrawal from society and its evils to inactivity in nature's realm. Thus, in contrast with the public service required of the Confucian gentleman, Daoism promoted a self-centred passivity. The ideal was to combine both *yang* and *yin*, that is an active urban

2 **Wilderness and the country retreat** Ming scroll painting.

career of public service during one's prime with a passive retirement to the country for the cultivation of harmony with the *dao* in old age.

Town and country planning

The ideals of Confucius and Laozi are reflected in the traditional Chinese approach to town and country planning respectively (see 1 and 2, pages 6 and 13). The earliest recorded Chinese garden, Lingtai, was laid out by the Zhou about the time of Laozi, but the earliest images of houses related organically to nature – in poetry and painting – are much later. The earliest record of Chinese town planning is also Zhou. The subject of a treatise (*Kao gong ji*) incorporated in its original form in the *Rituals of Zhou* (*Zhou li*) by the time of Confucius, the capital (Wangchang) was a walled square with three gates to each side linked by triads of avenues forming a grid. The imperial audience hall was to the fore (i.e. south), backed by residential pavilions (to its north) but, as imperial power was by nature centralised, later interpreters have placed the palace in the centre. The Temple of the Ancestors was to its east; the Altar of Earth to its west; the market to its north.

Contrary to the centralised nature of the square, however, *feng shui* dictated a southerly aspect to houses, palaces, temples and, therefore, to the town. *Feng shui* ('wind and water'), the prescription for rapport with nature, took on the mystical dimension of geomancy as natural phenomena and human behaviour – cosmic force and the imperial performance above all – were seen as interlinked. Worship of the spirits of natural phenomena naturally led to belief in the auspiciousness of topography and to the evolution of complex formulae for its divination, especially when concordances were discovered between the form of physical features and the configuration of the stars which governed the affairs of men. Nevertheless, *feng shui* is essentially practical: in China the north is the source of evil in the form of both rough weather and even rougher invaders, so the ideal site for town and building was south-sloping, exposed to the sun and drained to a protective river at its base, with an arc of hills to the north. Hence the axiality of Chinese planning. Hence, too, the invariable wall: around house, palace, temple, town, China.

Laozi inspired resignation to the incomprehensible irrationality of nature, but Confucius promoted har-

monisation with the order of nature. In harmony with
this order, everyone in Confucian society recognised
his place as one of subordination to the continuously
ascending line of authority culminating in the emperor,
the instrument of heaven's will. And in accord with the
linear hierarchy of state, as with *feng shui*, the principal elements of town, temple, palace and house naturally would be aligned on a south-north axis in
ascending order of importance – as in the image of the
imperial palace which incorporated the portrait of
Confucius (see 1, page 6). That post-dates the sage by
2000 years, but the principle is represented by the
Shang character for 'palace' (宮), if not quite so clearly
by the remains of the south-facing palace halls in their
seats near Luoyang, Zhengzhou and Anyang. The
south-facing palace in Luoyang, which Confucius visited in his peregrinations, evidently consisted of several pavilions ranged in order of importance – though
the excavators of the site, which was occupied for over
500 years, have not revealed a city quite as regular as
the *Kao gong ji* ideal.

Neither Confucius nor Laozi presented himself as
the prophet of a new religion. Neither offered consolation to the soul facing the uncertainty of death.

Indeed, Confucius spoke of 'heaven' not 'god' and declined to speak of death in man's imperfect knowledge of life or of the world of spirits while that of man needed attention. However, he did condone ancestor worship, though it followed from belief in the continued existence of the soul after physical death and the distinction between good and evil spirits – those honoured or neglected by their descendants – who could intervene positively or negatively in the lives of men.

The Qin and the Han

From the Warring States, who gave their name to the period after the fall of the Zhou, the Qin (from whom the name China is derived) had emerged predominant by 246 BC: exposed on the north-west frontier to the pressure of nomadic tribes,[3] they were hardened in the constant conflict and doubtless owed their devastating cavalry to superior horses won from the enemy. Ruthless in his determination to eliminate all opposition and to assert his authority, the king of Qin (also named Qin) abolished the Zhou feudal order and the states that had emerged from it, defined 36 provinces governed by his delegates and in 221 proclaimed himself the first emperor of China.

3 **Encampment of a tribal chief of the Han confederation known as Xiong-nü** scroll painting (Boston Museum of Fine Arts).

Qin's state was founded on the idea that order depends on law rather than a moral responsibility. The state's code of law was draconian and standardised throughout the empire, and any work promoting the idea that order might derive from morality, custom – widely varied in the domains constituting the empire – or any source other than the law was burned. As further instruments of unification Qin standardised the coinage and measurements, and imposed a single script on the many languages spoken in his vast domain. For the widespread dissemination of his imperial ideology he capitalised on the invention of paper – a by-product of silk, whose manufacture was well developed by his time. A network of roads and canals was also consolidated. Not least as a symbol, defining the borders of the empire at their most vulnerable, he built the Great Wall – or rather consolidated and extended existing ramparts of impacted earth for c. 5000 kilometres (3000 miles).[4] Qin also provided himself with one of the world's most amazing tombs.[5]

The very weight of its oppressiveness brought the regime down in peasant insurrection on Qin's death in 210 BC. By 206, power in the capital Chang'an

(Everlasting-peace) was in the hands of the Han. Building on Qin's foundations, while moderating his system, they gave China its model imperial edifice. The centralised monarchy was consolidated, but it was not long before the fief system was revived for members of the imperial family. And it was the Han who determined that their power was to be exercised through a bureaucracy established on Confucian lines. Moral responsibility supplanted Qin's legalism as the basis of order.

Public works were sustained, indeed Qin's Great Wall was extended and its width doubled in part, but effort was concentrated on roads and waterways, flood control and irrigation, which were seen as ben-

4 OVERLEAF **The Great Wall, near Badaling** the earth core has been exposed by dilapidation of a later revetment.

Following the example set by the Zhou, most of the warring states built sections of wall against the nomads – and one another. Qin's amalgamation produced a wall c. 10,000 *li* in length – which gave it its traditional name, *Wanli changcheng* (The Everlasting Great Wall). The wall reached most of its definitive length (twice that of the Qin dynasty) under the Han in the last two centuries BC.

5 **Qin ling (Qin's tomb)** trenches with the terracotta army.

The earliest tombs of the important Chinese were tumuli, usually circular, covering burial chambers in the form of a house or palace – accommodation for eternity matching the status of the temporal residence. Along with material possessions, retainers were sacrificed and interred with the Shang rulers, but the Zhou substituted ceramic figures for the people. Although legendary for his cruelty, Qin retained the surrogates – except for his wives and the workmen who knew the secrets of access to the burial chamber. As his

eficial by the vast mass of the people pressed into building them. The lengthening of the Great Wall protected
a trade route opened to the west from Chang'an, and
the empire was extended into central Asia to control
it at the cost of involvement with the nomads. China
was held to be largely self-sufficient but it sought jade,
with its mystical powers of preservation, and the fast,
strong horses of Ferghana. In return, the main export
was silk, and trade in this Chinese speciality ultimately
linked Chang'an with Rome – where the taste for silk
was virtually insatiable by the end of the reign of
Augustus in AD 14. Much other than silk flowed
through Asia with trade, of course – above all ideas.

army – especially his cavalry – had been his power base on
earth, his tomb had to be vast enough to contain some 9000
life-size terracotta models of its personnel and their horses
to sustain him for eternity in the palace below the centre of
his terraced pyramidal mound – 1700 metres (5600 feet) to
the west of the three pits containing the army and still 350
metres (1150 feet) wide and 45 metres (150 feet) high after
2000 years. The subterranean structure seems to have been
of wood: brick vaults were introduced to the tomb
chambers of his Han successors.

The imperial capitals

Qin's capital, long occupied, was to the north-west of modern Xi'an and on its elevation to the imperial seat it reputedly contained a palace for each of the states bound to the empire. However, the first emperor began a new palace city to the south of the old one, avowedly adopting the centralised ideal of Zhou Wangchang for it as a badge of imperium – and the point was certainly not lost on most of his successors. Little more remains than the great rectangular palace platform with its several granite column bases over 1 metre (3 feet 3 inches) in diameter.

Chang'an was further south. Though divided into walled districts (luli), unusually it does not seem to have been planned axially in a regular perimeter from the outset but to have developed irregularly around pre-existing palace compounds to embrace several additional palaces. In its southern suburb, however, formal planning was taken to a biaxial extreme in square ritual compounds.

Palaces and houses

Little survives of the palaces of Han Chang'an – other than their enclosures and rectangular podia of

6 Han palace hall with wings and towers Eastern Han
funerary relief (New York, Metropolitan Museum of Art).

A two-storey palatial hall is shown in several Han reliefs,
the upper level for the lord, the lower for the servants. Note
the brackets above the columns and the straight ridge of the
hipped roof. Houses of any stature, as here, seem also to
have had matching wings (called xiang in contemporary
records such as the *Shi ji*, written by the court historian of
the emperor Wudi, 140–87 BC). These were linked to
the short sides by bridge-like galleries. Beyond them were
towers, either for defence or for emblazoning with the
insignia of the lord – or both.

impacted earth – but there are images in relief of palace halls[6] and models of courtyard houses[7] and towers[8] backed by archaeological evidence. Doubtless reproducing the forms of the palaces in miniature, the model houses are usually axial with the main hall centred to the north of a court, smaller halls east and west, occasionally an even smaller one to the south, and often covered verandahs framing the court to link the halls. Like the free-standing towers, apparently common in the period, the main

7 **Han courtyard house** Eastern Han pottery funerary model (New York, Metropolitan Museum of Art).

The entrance (foreground), guarded by a dog, is overlooked by a watchtower (left), the tallest structure in the complex. The accommodation block, with open-fronted kitchen attached, is at the head of the court (background). The eastern range (right) consisted of a latrine above a pigsty, and a two-storey granary (almost as high as the watchtower). Inscribed bricks from early Han tombs in Shandong give a clear picture of double-courtyard houses.

The earliest Chinese calligraphy suggests that this type of courtyard plan was known as early as the Shang, and it is easily envisaged under the Zhou as responding to the

Confucian precepts of the hierarchically ordered extended family, but there is no archaeological evidence predating the Han. The earliest houses so far recovered in China, from the 4th millennium BC settlement at Banpo (near Xi'an), were circular and probably derived from the tent – though built of wattle and daub over pits. Later ones at the same site were rectangular, south-facing and built on a timber frame.

8 **Han tower** Eastern Han pottery funerary model (New York, Metropolitan Museum of Art).

Usually up to four storeys and popular as status symbols, towers were built for additional accommodation attached to houses and as observation posts – free-standing or as part of a complex for military and purely aesthetic purposes. The models show that the typical Chinese trabeated structural system, incorporating brackets, was familiar to the Han.

building was sometimes multi-storeyed (lou). Even at the popular level Confucian influence is apparent in the hierarchical ordering of domestic forms, and the microcosm of the house reproduces the macrocosm of the city.

Expansion of the empire and its infrastructure had its cost: the winning of territory boosted military power; increased taxation impoverished the peasants and vast estates were consolidated at their expense by magnates; and concessions to secure the allegiance of the magnates sapped the power of the centre. Under increasing pressure from the nomads, excited by the route to the west, the capital was moved from Chang'an to Luoyang early in the 1st century AD – and was built as a near-rectangle with the main axis north–south and rectangular northern and southern palace compounds. The Han dynasty survived for another two centuries until c. 200 when, eclipsed by the magnates and ridden by factions manipulated by concubines and eunuchs, its corrupt court fell prey to a rabble army of dispossessed peasants. Lacking leaders able to construct a new imperial regime, the rabble – and the empire – dissolved into chaos and confusion.

9 Dunhuang, The Pure Land of the Western Paradise
7th-century fresco.

The Western Paradise, which Amitabha offered as
salvation to those whose absolute faith in him is expressed
through worship, is represented as a palace in deference to
the royal (and Western) origins of Siddhartha Gautama,

The rise of Buddhism

Confucius and Laozi had sought ways out of their period of confusion with reason and discipline, mysticism and licence respectively. However complementary in their appeal to the sense and sensibility of the living, offering little consolation to the soul in torment at the prospect of death, both left an emotional void. And the chaos that followed the fall of the Han, inimical to faith in the old order, sharpened the torment.

During the two centuries of chaos the salving ideal of Mahayana Buddhism filled the void. The Mahayana (Great Vehicle) postulated that grace was emitted by a multiplicity of Buddhas through the intercession of bodhisattvas – angels whose essence was the enlightenment of a Buddha and who had earned release from the burden of existence but whose compassion for suffering humanity had led them to

born to a prince of the Sakya clan on the border of India and Nepal, who attained Buddhahood with his enlightenment under the bodhi tree at Gaya in modern Bihar (see volume 5, INDIA AND SOUTH-EAST ASIA, page 23). The palace belongs to the type, illustrated in Han reliefs, with a central hall linked to wings by bridge-like galleries (see 6, page 27).

renounce the goal of Buddhahood in offering to transfer their own merit to their devotees. Not surprisingly, the Chinese were devoted to the Amitabha Buddha, the Lord of the Pure Land of the Western Paradise to which he admitted those with faith in him,[9] and to his ministering angel, the Bodhisattva Avalokiteshvara, personified in China in female terms as Guanyin.

As an alternative to faith in the transference of merit from bodhisattva to devotee, the Chinese also developed the concept of the Chan (popular in Japan as Zen), which admitted the possibility of personal enlightenment through a spiritual yoga. Moreover, in the light of the transformation of the Buddha from great teacher to god and under the inspiration of ancestor worship, Confucius and Laozi were gradually seen at least as quasi-divine, and faith in any one of the three was deemed compatible with faith in the others – though there was never one canonical Daoist creed.

Post-Han China, in common with the period following the Zhou, consisted of many warring states. The Han empire broke into three main kingdoms: Wei in the north, with one of the ancient Warring States as its nucleus and its capital at Luoyang; Wu in the centre-south with its capital at Nanjing; and Shu in the

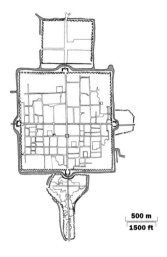

500 m
1500 ft

10 **Datong** 494–534, plan.

The first capital of the Northern Wei, Datong was strategically placed for a garrison to control the territory between the parallel ranges of the Great Wall bequeathed by the Han. On the basis of much later accounts it is thought to have had a square enclosure, but remains are scanty.

south-west. To internecine rivalry was added nomadic invasion, most assertively by the Tabgatch (or Toba) Tartars. Late in the 4th century they won Datong[10] and the northern Wei territory from the Han tribe of the ancient fiefdom of Jin, acquired the name of the territory and went on to reassemble something of a respectable empire in the north. Ruling first from Datong then from Luoyang[11] after 494, they fostered Buddhism – and great monasteries were carved from

11 **Luoyang** 494–534, plan.

On moving to Luoyang in 494, the Northern Wei extended the old Han capital (which had been 9 *li* long and 6 *li* wide) to 15 by 20 *li* (according to a description of 547). The remains of the southern palace compound were suppressed and the northern palace was rebuilt to a larger scale: the one-palace city was henceforth the imperial norm as it had originally been the Zhou imperial ideal – though that, of course, was square rather than rectangular. A grid of streets, interrupted only by the palace compound towards the centre, defined numerous wards (220 according to the description of 547). The reason for the vast expansion of the city area was the growth of the Buddhist community and its monasteries under Northern Wei patronage.

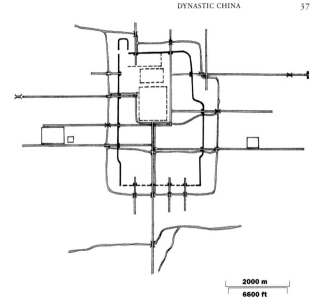

2000 m
6600 ft

the rock near each of these capitals. The rulers of Jin had expanded from Luoyang south into the kingdom of Wu and took its capital c. 280. They abandoned their northern seat, and regrouped around Nanjing where they also encouraged the Buddhists – so much so that there were reputedly 480 temples in Wu by the middle of the 6th century. North and south, the capitals conformed more or less to the rectangular norm, with the palace at the head of the main north–south axis, and garrisoned Datong was as regular in its geometry as any of its Roman counterparts.

The Sui and the triumph of the Tang

There were, of course, other contenders for predominance – north and south – and in the subsequent reunification of China, the Sui (581–618) and the Tang (618–907) echo the history of the Qin and Han: a brutal determination to construct, or reconstruct, the empire followed by moderation in running it. While Qin was obsessed with throwing the Great Wall around his empire to assert its integrity, the Sui expended millions of lives on the equally gargantuan task of extending the Grand Canal to bind the empire within. A peasant revolt followed the humiliating

defeat of the Sui's attempt to conquer Korea. As usual
the peasants produced no leader, but a magnate capitalised on the situation to claim the mandate of heaven
– and he won popular support with the equitable redis-
tribution of land. Emulating Han achievement, his
Tang dynasty was to take Chinese civilisation to its
apogee. The bureaucracy was restored and refined,
and its growth was certainly not inhibited by the invention of printing. Central Asia was resecured, Korea
finally conquered and even Japan succumbed to the
cultural hegemony of Chang'an, re-established by the
Sui as the capital, and under the Tang, by the end of
the 7th century, the greatest city on earth.

   Sui Chang'an was unprecedented in its obsessive
order[12] and the Tang perfected it with palaces and
tombs of unrivalled magnificence.[13,15] In the Buddhist
art of Tang, China the Pure Land was usually represented as the Palace of the Western Paradise in allu-
sion to the royal origin of the Buddha, and the model
was surely the emperor's palace at Chang'an. Conforming to the type most commonly represented in the
Tang frescos of the Buddhist grottoes at Dunhuang,
for example (see 9, page 32), the excavated remains of the
Chang'an palace reveal a great podium supporting a

12 **Chang'an, Imperial City** plan based on archaeological evidence and using details from a stele engraving of 1080.

In 582 the Sui established a new capital, Daxing, to the south of Han Chang'an, where central Xi'an is now, and reproduced it in part at Luoyang of the Northern Wei c. 605 (see 11, page 37). Eighty-four square kilometres (52 square miles) in area, Daxing was slightly longer east–west than north–south, like Luoyang, but the authority of the north–south axis had never been more assertive nor the discipline of the grid clearer. The broad central avenue led to the Imperial City (containing administration areas, the imperial ancestral temple and sacrificial altars) beyond which was the Sui palace city (for the emperor and his entourage). One hundred and eight walled districts, devised to control the population and graded in size according to occupation, were symmetrically disposed about the axis. Even the eastern and western markets (the latter specifically for foreign traders plying the Silk Road) were matched in site and scale. Only the lake of Fuyong yuan (Imperial Peony Garden) in the south-east corner pushed the perimeter wall beyond a pure rectangle.

The palaces of the main imperial compound, dominating the whole from its central position with its back to the northern wall, were rebuilt by the Tang (who recalled the

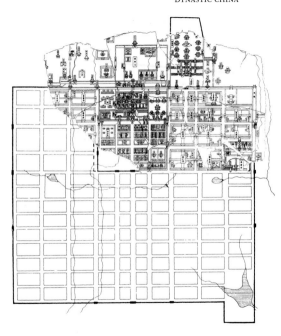

name Chang'an) and the new Daming palace was developed
from 634 in a park laid out by the Sui beyond the north-east
section of the city wall. This was the emperor's main seat
from 663 until it was destroyed by fire at the end of the 9th
century. Archaeological evidence and later representations
on scrolls show that both palaces had great halls aligned
on the north–south axis. The first ceremonial hall of the
Daming complex, 600 metres (2000 feet) beyond the gate,
was the Hanyuan dian with its symmetrical wings; the
second was 300 metres (1000 feet) farther north; the
residential pavilion was 95 metres (310 feet) farther north
still. An adjunct to the west, identified as the Linde dian
(Hall of the Righteous Unicorn), seems to have been a
banqueting hall whose central pavilion was flanked by
symmetrical wings with a pair of subsidiary blocks before
and behind them. The Xingqing gong, towards the centre
of the east side, was built in the first half of the 8th century
and was subsequently assigned to the empress dowager.

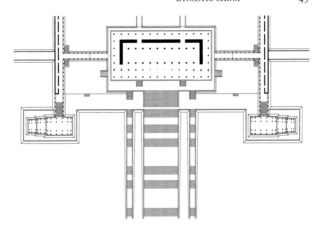

13 **Chang'an, Daming Imperial Palace, Hanyuan dian
(Hall of Embodying the Way)** plan reconstructed from
excavations.

14 **Jiucheng, palace** detail of a Qing scroll painting on silk, 1691 (New York, Metropolitan Museum of Art).

Founded by the Sui and rebuilt by the Tang as a summer palace, Jiucheng was destroyed more than 500 years before the Qing era and is recreated with imagination informed by a long history of eulogy.

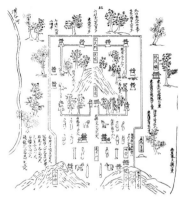

15 Chang'an, Qian ling of the Gaozong emperor
(650–83) 14th-century view based on an 11th-century survey for the Song *Chang'an zhi* (*Record of Chang'an*).

The Tang emulated the Han in the size and splendour of their tombs. The old formula was retained, including a subterranean palace, but the greatest of the Tang emperors selected sites with natural mounds and formed their several vaulted chambers with brick, like many of the Han. Most impressive is the Qian ling and its 'spirit way': the avenue of approach from the south lined with symbolic creatures.

central hall linked to side pavilions by colonnaded galleries. So too does the portrait of the Tang palace, Jiucheng, outside Chang'an[14] – an earthly paradise if there ever was one.

The Tang demise also followed the Han pattern, but the Buddhist monasteries rivalled the magnates in the amassing of great estates at the expense of the peasantry – and the imperial treasury. The monasteries were suppressed in 845, when the economy was on the verge of collapse. Daoism was promoted officially and it took on more of the nature of a religion, but the popularity of Buddhism survived. So too did the secular magnates, and the regime staggered on for only about another 50 years, overawed by the great landlords, destabilised by popular unrest.

The Song

Chaos was relatively short lived before the advent of the Song (960–1274) – a brilliant, if lax and unmilitaristic, dynasty that furthered Tang achievement in the arts. They disputed the north with the Khitan Mongols, who established their Liao dynasty at Datong in 907 but were overwhelmed by the Jurchen Tartars early in the 12th century. Taking the name of

16 **Suzhou** plan, rubbing from a stone engraving of 1229 after a map drawn by the geographer Huang Shang in 1193 (London, British Library).

Founded in the 6th century BC, more than a millennium later Suzhou was the centre of the silk industry and the hub of China's waterway system at the junction of the lower Yangtze and the Grand Canal. The perimeter walls (rectangular except for three canted corners) were breached by five gates that were doubled for land- and water-borne traffic. The canonical grid, depending on three gates to each side of a square, is consequently impractical, and the walled districts disappear, but order subsists in the alignment of all the main arteries (streets and canals) to the cardinal points. Further, in consequence of the pre-eminence of the south-western gate and the arteries running north from it, unmatched to the east, the innermost rectangle of the imperial enclosure is dislocated to the south-east of centre.

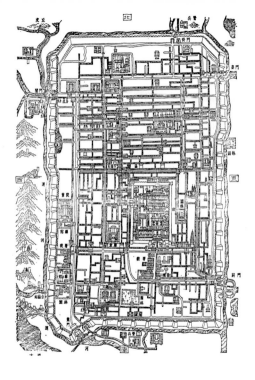

the ancient state of Jin, the latter forced the Song to retreat from their north-central capital Kaifeng to a new southern capital at Hangzhou in 1127 – despite the Chinese invention of gunpowder. The Song brought garden design in particular to unexcelled heights there. From there too, having lost control of the great western trade route to the Mongols, the Song were well placed to develop maritime links with their south-east Asian neighbours.

Kaifeng, Hangzhou and Suzhou, the last a provincial centre, honoured the ancient planning tradition if only in the breach. The plan of Suzhou[16] incised on a Song stone tablet, the earliest such document yet identified in China, is a near-rectangle with an odd number of gates and an irregular grid of streets or canals that may still be traced on site.

Kublai Khan and Lamaism

The Mongols triumphed under Ghingis Khan's grandson, Kublai, in a variation of the usual pattern of change, and subjected China to their regime, known as Yuan, from 1279 to 1368. Kublai extended the boundaries of the empire to include parts of Tibet, hitherto rarely a political unit but subscribing in the

17 OVERLEAF **Samye, Tibet, monastery** early 19th-century painting (Newark Museum).

Evolved with sacrificial rituals to support the divine right of the isolated Himalayan plateau's earliest kings (1st century BC), the native religion was challenged by Buddhism after an unprecedented era of dynastic expansion unified Tibet and won an empire extending beyond the plateau early in the 7th century. The Buddhist states engaged by the Tibetans in northern India provided models for empire, and the moral imperative of the Buddha's ideal of universal salvation provided an effective imperial bond – as many emperors in the Indian orbit had found. The development of Lamaism may be traced from the foundation of Samye, Tibet's first Buddhist monastery, by the greatest emperor Trisong Detsen (755–97) for his Indian guru, the Tantric priest Padma Sambhava.

With Buddhism came much that was endemic to Indian civilisation, especially monasticism. The seats of both faith and learning, the monasteries soon became rich and powerful enough to challenge the traditional ruling class, and bitter reaction led to the persecution of the Buddhists in the 9th century – as in the contemporary Tang empire. The Buddhist ruler was assassinated and the state disintegrated. Attempting to consolidate control, however, the adherents of the old religion found Buddhist precepts so essential to the state that they were forced to borrow them. Compromised, they were no match for a counter-offensive launched by a descendant of the last Buddhist ruler with a faith rejuvenated in India. That faith was principally the messianic Buddhism of the Vajrayana (Way of the Thunderbolt), which allowed magical formulae (by no means foreign to animists like the old believers) and esoteric practices (Tantras, involving the ritual breaching of sexual and other taboos) to accelerate the otherwise protracted evolutionary process of personal release enshrined in the salvation ideal.

With the destruction of Buddhism in India following the Muslim invasions of the late 12th century, many refugees took a wide range of Buddhist beliefs and practices to Tibet. From the ferment, the masters (lamas) in their monasteries (lamaseries) distilled several orders of Lamaism – four orders are recognised, one predating the persecution. It was the post-persecution order of the Sakya monastery, founded to define dogma and regulate the institutions of revived Buddhism in Tibet, that converted Kublai Khan. By the mid-14th century the most prominent order was the Geluk: it developed its largest monasteries around the old Jokhang shrine at Lhasa and produced the line of Dalai Lamas.

main to the idiosyncratic amalgam of an ancient occult
animism and various strands of Tantric Buddhism
known as Lamaism.[17] The Tibetans coalesced under
one of the principal lamas to meet the Mongol threat.
His emissary so impressed Kublai in debate with
Christians, Muslims and Chinese theologians that
Lamaism was adopted as the official religion of the
Yuan state, and a Tibetan monument was erected over
the new capital Beijing.[18] The legendary savagery of
the Mongols was somewhat moderated by the
influence of Buddhism under Kublai – and even in
its abstruse Lamaist form Buddhism was again
considered consistent with Confucianism.

The capital, moved to the north-eastern site of
Beijing – nearer Mongolia – was built in rather stricter
conformity to the tradition descending from the Zhou
than the laxer Song cities of the south. Foreign

18 **Beijing, Miaoying si (Temple of the Miraculous
Response), dagoba** 1271.

A reliquary stupa of the Tibetan bulbous form (as distinct
from the typical Indian hemispherical one), this is the major
surviving monument of Kublai's reign – indeed of the whole
Yuan period of building in Beijing.

dominance was nevertheless intolerable to the proud Chinese, and tribal dissension among the second generation of Kublai's successors opened the way for the inevitable peasant revolt.

The Ming and the Qing

This time, uniquely, the peasants produced a leader capable of assuming the mandate of heaven in 1368. He rejected the Yuan capital for Nanjing, but his successors moved back to Beijing in 1402.[19] Assuming the epithet Ming (Bright), the new dynasty not only followed the usual pattern of national renewal, redistributing the land, renovating the roads, canals and urban defences,[20,21] reinforcing the Great Wall against

19 **Beijing** 19th-century engraving, plan.
   (1) Tartar city; (2) Imperial City; (3) Forbidden City (Imperial Palace); (4) Chinese city; (5) Tian tan (Temple of Heaven); (6) Xiannong tan (Temple of Agriculture).

Open to well-watered plains to the south and encircled by hills to the north – as *feng shui* requires – the site was settled at least as early as the Zhou and was developed as the capital of one of the Warring States (as Yanjing, 'Capital of Swallows'). A trade centre and base for expeditions

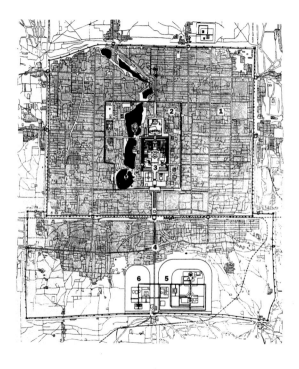

against Korea from the Han to the Tang, it fell to various nomadic tribes before the Yuan took it from the Jin and established it as a base (Khanbalik, 1215). Enclosing an extensive grazing area for horses, the later Yuan capital was longer on the north–south axis than east–west (rather than square in accordance with Zhou prescription) and there were 11 rather than 12 gates (only two to the north). The main streets linked opposite gates except where the impenetrable imperial compound interposed itself. As at Suzhou (see 16, page 49), this was south of the centre but its main gate was aligned with the central gate in the southern wall, and the two were linked by a particularly grand ceremonial avenue.

Inheriting a site devastated in the struggle against the Yuan, the Ming pruned the northern districts with their protected grazing areas, so reducing the extent of the wall and the number of gates (to nine), made the north–south axis shorter than the east–west one, and placed the Imperial Palace enclosure closer to the centre. This displaced the working and living areas of artisans and traders – leaving the city primarily to those associated with the workings of the government – and a new commercial and industrial suburb was built to the south of the city around the compound of the Tian tan.

20 Xi'an, wall.

The massive walls of Beijing were destroyed by the Communists in 1958. Nanjing's wall was the longest in the world and survives in part: it was atypical in conforming to the hilly contours of the site rather than to the rationalist ideal. The wall at Xi'an gives perhaps the best image of the massiveness and inexorability of Ming urban defences.

21 Xi'an, bell tower (foreground) and drum tower.
Every major Chinese city had a drum tower to mark the hours of day and night, and a bell tower to announce the opening and closing of the city gates and to alert the population at times of danger. These recall the walled Han courtyard house with its watchtower (see 7, page 29).

22 Jiayuguan, fort, inner court and watchtower 1372.

At the western extremity of the Great Wall, guarding part of the Gansu Corridor (the narrow pass into which the province of Gansu extends westwards), the fort has a series of courts covering 33,500 square metres (360,600 square feet), enclosed by earthworks up to 10 metres (33 feet) in height and overlooked by watchtowers (renovated from 1988). Its complexity and size notwithstanding, the descent of the form from the prototype of the Han courtyard house (see 7, page 29) could hardly be clearer – nor could its further expansion to the scale of the walled city with its towered gates and, above all, its drum and bell towers.

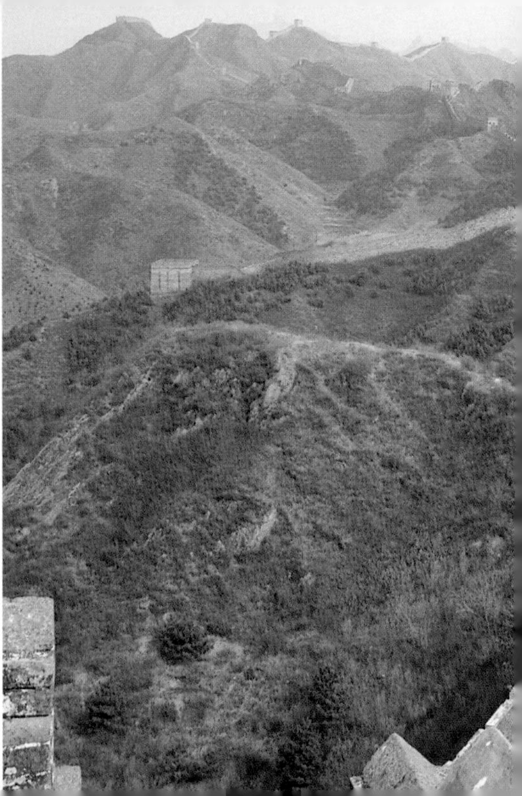

a repetition of the Mongol invasions[22,23] and reasserting authority in central Asia, but also it developed sea-borne trade. It conformed to the usual pattern of decline too, though now the stultification of the bureaucracy through the arch-conservatism of the examination system was a key factor. Not innovative in the arts, the Ming devoted their most significant efforts to restoration and rebuilding on a grandiose scale – and little of China's heritage of traditional architecture in fact predates the Ming or even their successors, the Qing (1644–1911).

The Ming fell in the usual way – an effete court controlled by corrupt and rapacious eunuchs, bankrupted by land and tax concessions to the magnates, and toppled by peasant revolt. And the peasants lost the initiative in the usual way. Filling the void, the Qing – the 'Pure', the last of China's imperial dynasties – descended from Manchuria. Though aloof from the subjected Chinese, they restored Chinese institutions. Like the Ming, they produced several effective emperors who expended great resources on reasserting Chi-

23 PREVIOUS PAGES **Jinshanling, The Great Wall** Ming revetment, 15th century.

24 Chengde, Bishu Shan Zhuang (Mountain Hamlet for Escape from Summer Heat, Hebei).

Not to forget the vigour of his hunting forebears, the Qing Kangxi emperor (1662–1722) had a palace built in the valley of Chengde as a base both for sport and for maintaining the close relationship with the Mongols on which Manchu power depended. Temples built on the slopes around the imperial enclosure, and aligned with it on radial axes, catered for the esoteric beliefs of the tribesmen. The resort allowed the court to escape the heat of Beijing in the summer and provided for hunting in the autumn from 1703 until the death of the Jiaqing emperor there in 1820.

25 **Lhasa, Tibet, view with Potala Palace** 19th-century painting (Toronto, Royal Ontario Museum).

The seat of the Dalai Lama, the Potala (centre) is evoked as the Palace of the Pure Land of the Western Paradise. The Dalai Lama is shown returning to it from the Jokhang temple (right foreground) – the advance guard having already reached the main gate with its typically Tibetan stupas. Founded by the first of Tibet's Buddhist rulers in the mid-7th century, the Jokhang is Tibet's holiest temple, housing the nation's holiest icons – reputedly brought to the king by his Nepalese and Chinese queens. The three complexes in the background are the main monasteries of the area – Drepung, Sera and Ganden, all founded at the beginning of the 15th century. Drepung (left) was the seat of the Dalai Lama until Potala was built in the mid-17th century. Rebuilt on 8th-century foundations by the fifth Dalai Lama under the vigorous Kangxi, the south-facing complex is divided into two contiguous parts. The Red Palace in the centre (and its adjuncts to the west) contains monastic prayer halls and cells associated with shrines to the Buddha and past Dalai Lamas. The White Palace to the east provided the accommodation and reception halls of the Dalai Lama. The monumental steps from the compound, which rise steeply from the edge of the town to the south,

penetrate the massive substructure and divide to provide the
principal access to each part – the west fork leads directly to
the Red Palace through a central cryptoportico, while the
east fork leads to a circuitous interior passage and thence
to the forecourt of the east-facing White Palace.

nese authority wherever it had been exercised before, and on sustaining or exceeding the monuments to imperial grandeur produced by their predecessors.

As outsiders the Qing felt some affinity to the Yuan and maintained the Yuan capital, Beijing, as the Ming had done. To mollify the Mongols they built another seat at Chengde,[24] on the hilly edge of their Manchurian homeland, as a monument to the unity of the nations under them. Greatly expanding the empire into Tibet,[25] they saw considerable political advantage in reviving Yuan patronage of Lamaism, and the Tibetan contribution to Chengde is a major ingredient in the synthesis to which the regime aspired. Yet they were obdurate in sustaining the traditional belief in the superiority of all things Chinese. The Qing's humiliation in the 19th century at the hands of the Europeans and the accession of Nationalist, Socialist and Communist regimes in the wake of popular uprisings at the beginning of the 20th century are beyond the scope of this book.

Though Chinese civilisation is venerable and its architectural tradition one of the world's longest living ones, few Chinese buildings are very old – even Qin's Great Wall survives only in its 15th-century revetment (see 23, pages 62–3). Reliefs and the clay models interred with the dead record the domestic types of the Han (see 6–8, pages 27–30), but their buildings are now lost. Though often based on stone and walled in brick, perishable timber was the main material – and the buildings have suffered no less than others with the fortunes of their patrons. Age was not in itself venerated and buildings were readily destroyed or rebuilt on a grander scale as the regime's favour fluctuated.

If not the material substance of buildings, however, the form of Chinese architecture descends intact – or without fundamental change – from time immemorial. The conservative order of the Confucian tradition, materialised largely by anonymous builders in accordance with manuals, ensured this. And fundamental to order in Chinese building was a trabeated structural system with standard parts, dictated by physical necessity but defined by mathematical ratios, determining standard units of space and volume. Multiplied, these usually constituted a hypostyle hall scaled in accordance with the rank of the patron. The structure needed protection from the weather and dampness: hence a raised masonry podium and an overhanging timber roof – both also strictly graded in height in accordance with the rank of the patron.

The earliest traces of a timber hypostyle hall on a brick and stone podium have been detected in the remains of Anyang, the capital of the earliest of China's historical dynasties, the Shang. Standardisation is apparent in the conception of space, but the nature of the remains leaves definition by mathematical ratios only to be surmised. Likewise, the form of roof may also only be guessed at but, when it does appear, the traditional form recalls the tent from which building often takes its departure (see 3, pages 18–19).

Indian influences

The earliest images of a Chinese building appear well over a millennium later than the Shang in the Han reliefs and models, then in the works of the Buddhists five centuries later still. When Buddhism arrived from India, however, it naturally brought its architectural tradition with it. Among the remains of the long-abandoned desert city of Gaochang, on the great trade

26 **Gaochang, Buddhist temple** 6th century?, partial
reconstruction.

The typical Indian Buddhist shrine had a hall with
ambulatory for ritual circumambulation about a sacred

object (chaitya). At first this was a stupa, but images of the Buddha and bodhisattvas emerged predominant with the development of the Mahayana. Once accommodating such images here, the central feature conforms to the type represented by the superstructure (shikhara) of early Indian temples like the one at Bodh Gaya (see volume 5, INDIA AND SOUTH-EAST ASIA, pages 79–80).

From its earliest representations in the embellishment of Buddhist monuments, the Indian temple is conceived as the palace of the gods. Modelled on the palace of the king, it consists of two main parts: a columned hall (mandapa) for audience (or for the faithful to await the manifestation of grace which is the divine equivalent of admission into the royal aura) and a multi-storey residential block (prasada) accommodating the royal entourage or the many aspects of the deity. The origin of the shikhara, the form was typical of all substantial residences, including the monastery where the columned hall was generally a sacred object house (chaitya-griha) and the multi-storey residential block was called vimana, the main element of a temple.

The great Chinese Buddhist pilgrim Xuanzang stayed in Gaochang on his way to India in 630 and returned by it 16 years later.

route through remote Xinjiang along which Buddhist missionaries penetrated east, is a brick temple with raised base and walled compound providing for ritual circumambulation (pradakshina) about a niched tower.[26] This recalls Indian prototypes both in general distribution and in the particular form of the multi-storey residential block.

Deeper into China, the earliest surviving, free-standing Buddhist shrines are rare stone cells with sculpted slab façades[27] representing the primitive vernacular structure of the Buddhist homeland. Earlier still are the first shrines of the series cut from the cliffs at Dunhuang, Longmen and Yungang.[28-32] Indian influence is apparent immediately in the basic conception of the rock-cut monastery and, later, in the multi-storey pier in the centre of the more complex works. In the architectural detail, moreover, the vernacular of the Buddhist homeland is represented but so too is the native Chinese structural system.

The pagoda

Apart from stone-cut shrines and perhaps the brick temples of Xinjiang, the oldest buildings in China are several brick pagodas built as repositories for relics or

27 **Buddhist stone shrine** late 6th-century Sui? (New York, Metropolitan Museum of Art).

Other surviving examples, such as one on Mount Fang, have tiered roofs like miniature pagodas.

28 Dunhuang, Mogao excavated Buddhist monastic complex mid-4th century.

The remotest of Han provincial outposts in an oasis on the Silk Road at the edge of the southern extension of the Gobi Desert, Dunhuang was the first Chinese settlement to support Buddhist monks in considerable numbers. The influence of Bamiyan (west along the great trade route, in modern Afghanistan) is immediately apparent in the incorporation of colossal images of the Buddha, but the ultimate source for the rock-cut Buddhist monastery is found in India's Barabar hills and the Western Ghats. Excavation of living rooms and shrines began soon after the mid-4th century and continued until the end of the 10th century. Simple cells at first, generally with tent-shaped roofs, they were later filled with icons primarily in fresco but also in sculpture (mainly stucco). Those of the Wei are among China's oldest masterpieces in both media, and they are rare survivals of the depredations of the anti-Buddhist, 9th-century Tang and then of more than a millennium of oblivion. There were also special repositories for documents and those recovered include the world's earliest surviving printed ones.

The screen (peifang) marks entry to a sacred site here, but it could be used before palaces and for commemoration in a secular context.

29 **Longmen, Guyang dong** begun c. 495.

The Buddhist excavation in the cliff by the river Yi at Longmen – some 12 kilometres (7 miles) south of Luoyang – was begun when the Northern Wei moved their capital to the old Imperial City in 494 and continued through all the imperial dynasties until the Qing. The earliest is the Guyang dong where a structural sacred object house of the apsidal form common in India continues the tradition of rich stone-cut relief established at Yungang (but in finer limestone) and furthers the ordering of the images begun in the latest work at the earlier site.

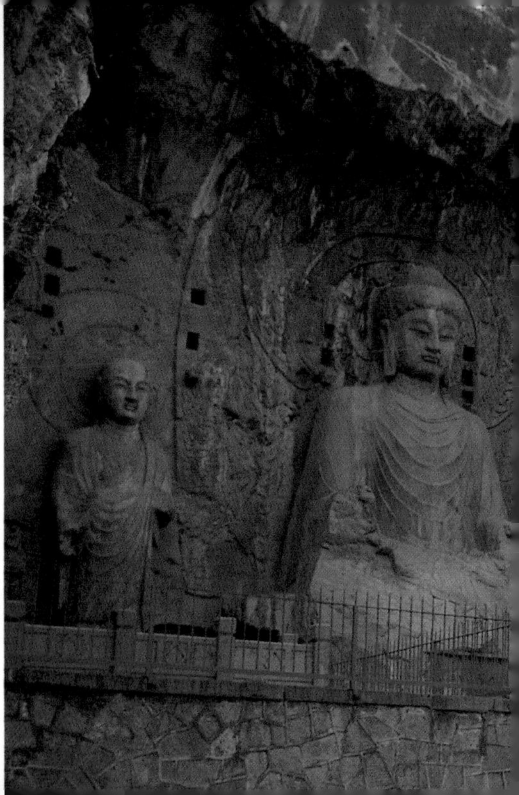

30 PREVIOUS PAGES **Longmen, Juxian (Honour to Forebears) cave** 672.

The 17-metre (56-foot) high image of Buddha Vairocana in the centre of the Juxian shrine (where there was once a wooden hall), flanked by the disciples Ananda and Kasyapa, bodhisattvas and guardians, represents the high point of Tang monumental stone sculpture.

31 **Yungang, Shrine 12** images in a trabeated hall.

Excavation in the sandstone cliff of Tianlong shan – some 16 kilometres (10 miles) west of Datong – began c. 450 under the patronage of the Northern Wei, and it reached its peak just before the emperor left Datong for Luoyang in 494. Work rapidly declined thereafter, but it seems to have ceased altogether only c. 525. Roughly rectangular, most of the so-called caves have a wealth of scenes from the life of the Buddha, bodhisattvas and other attendants carved into their walls – many betraying Hellenistic ancestry like those of Afghanistan and Gandhara (the heartland of the Buddhist Kushan empire in modern Pakistan).

The earlier excavators provided for ritual circum-ambulation around a central figure of the Buddha. Later

a many-tiered, many-niched tower related to the one in the temple at Gaochang (see 26, page 71) was not infrequent. That translated the Indian multi-storey residential block into Chinese – at least in part. Elsewhere the representation of icons in columned halls as here, an increasingly common practice with the growth in image-worship during the 5th century, provides the earliest surviving evidence of the fully developed native trabeated tradition whose origins were traced in the denuded platforms of Shang Anyang.

The representation of the structural prototype as a façade, common in India, distinguishes the main shrine at Tianlong shan (Heavenly Dragon Mountain, c. 560). It combines traditional Chinese trabeation with the ogee arch derived from the bowed bamboo of the Gangetic vernacular, as here but without the roof detail. As often in Mahayana India, too, a columned portico and contracted vestibule lead to a square hall with images in niches on the three inner sides.

32 Yungang, Shrine 11, central niche tower and prasada wall (right).

sacred texts (sutras) on the holy mountain of the
He'nan Song Shan. The Chinese, like many others, felt
nearer to god on a mountain – especially as 'god' meant
'heaven' in the main stream of the Confucian tradition.
As we know, moreover, Confucius was as dedicated to
the authority of *feng shui*, of order in submission to
cosmic forces, as Laozi was resigned to its irrationality in wild nature. Buddhists were diverse enough to
acquire the yen for both as the main strands of Chinese belief were interwoven.

The reliquary pagoda, enshrining the remains of
prominent proponents of the faith as in India, doubtless appeared in China with the earliest Buddhists – or
rather with their disappearance. The Tibetan lamas
ultimately provided the preferred model (see 17, page 53)
but the early monks of the Song Shan imported the
form of the Mahayana stupa with its many-tiered
umbrella (chattravali), popular not only in the Buddhist holy land but also particularly in the great
Kushan empire which covered much of central Asia
when Buddhism first entered.

Venerable as the reliquaries of the Holy Mountain
are, the oldest of the Song Shan pagodas is generally
thought to be the Songyue si (Song Peak)[33-34] built

under the Northern Wei c. 523 to house sutras brought from India. Anticipated as the hub of circumambulation in the centre of the later Yungang shrines – if not in the temple at Gaochang (see 26, page 71) – this form of pagoda is clearly a cross between the primitive Indian shikhara (which represents the multi-storey structure of the Gods) and the traditional Chinese tower (see 7, page 29). The polygonal precedent set by the Wei was most commonly followed under later dynasties, elaborated occasionally in timber but usually with simulated structural detail in masonry (see 50, 57–59, 70, pages 117, 127–131, 145). An enduring rectangular alternative, promoted under the Tang, translated the Mahabodhi temple at Bodh Gaya (see volume 5, INDIA AND SOUTHEAST ASIA, page 23) into Chinese terms with varying degrees of homage (see 32, page 83).[35]

The temple complex

The Dayan ta (Great Goose Pagoda) on the main axis of the Dacien si (Temple of Great Goodwill, founded in 647 by the future Tang Gaozong emperor) at

33 OVERLEAF **Song Shan, forest of pagodas with reliquary stupa (right).**

34 Song Shan, Songyue si sutra pagoda, traditionally
dated to 523.

The 12-sided, 39-metre (130-foot) high Songyue si,
whose curve anticipates that later developed in the Indian
prototype and the typical Khmer form, has been identified
as the oldest surviving free-standing structure in China. The
brickwork of plinth, drum and 15-tier superstructure was
probably plastered and painted predominantly in creamy
white. There is a chamber inside. Most other early pagodas
have six or eight sides.

35 Beijing, Zhenjue si (Temple of Enlightenment), entrance front late 15th century.

Built in the compound of a temple founded to house five golden statues of the Buddha and a model of the Mahabodhi temple at Bodh Gaya presented to the Ming Yongle emperor, a major shikhara rises from four smaller ones as on the original Mahabodhi temple at Bodh Gaya (see volume 5, INDIA AND SOUTH-EAST ASIA, page 79). Tang precedents for this relatively late work have been detected in the ruins of Jiaohe.

Xi'an is the greatest of the square sutra towers built under the Tang, embellished solely with the representation of trabeation, it marks the apogee of classical order.[36] And inside is a classic image of a temple hall.[37] Sutra pagodas were invariably associated with prayer halls in temple complexes – on axis, as here, though the original hall has gone.

The combination of single-storey hall and multi-storey tower reproduces the Indian palace of the

36 Xi'an, Dacien si, Dayan ta c. 700.

Mysteriously named and built to house documents brought from India by the Chinese Buddhist pilgrim Xuanzang in 652, the pagoda was enlarged and heightened from five to seven storeys from 701 – rooms on several levels allowed for storage of perishable documents away from the dampness of the ground. The extra three storeys were added from 766.

The representation of trabeation on the walls follows the precedent set by the stone-cut pagodas in several Yungang shrines (see 31–32, pages 81–83) and was anticipated in the five-storey pagoda built to enshrine Xuanzang's remains in 669. The ground-floor chamber preserves contemporary inscriptions and reliefs.

37 **Xi'an, Dacien si, Dayan ta** relief of a temple hall situated on a ground-floor lintel.

gods, of course, but in general the Chinese Buddhists built in the secular Chinese tradition. Their temples consisted of courts and halls, like the earliest houses known from the funerary models (see 7, page 29): indeed, many were palaces or houses in origin. Apart from the pagodas, they were also of traditional carpentry – never of monumental masonry as in India – and precious little survives from six or seven centuries of unimpeded growth in adherents and wealth of the faith to which they were dedicated. Indeed, the dissolution of the monasteries by the late Tang involved the destruction of almost all the prayer-halls from the period in which architecture was brought to a peak of refinement.

The temple hall

If not the oldest image of a temple hall, the early 8th-century Tang relief in the Dayan ta of the Dacien si is the most comprehensive early record. On a rectangular podium, the trabeated hall has five bays defined by six columns and is backed by a wall. Intermediate columns appear at the sides, implying the doubling of the bays in depth, but are omitted from the interior to accommodate the Buddha and his entourage. 'Lost column' plans were characteristic of Chinese halls. Equally characteristic is the widening of the central bay of the longitudinal range and the standardisation of the others. Incidentally, though the main entrance was generally through the central bay of the court, it was not stressed in any way other than widening – apart from the name tablet.

The back wall may have shared in bearing the load but that was not its primary role: as distinct as skin and bone, in principle the wall was protective, the column supportive. In this the latter was assisted by the bracket, the principal distinguishing feature of Chinese trabeation (see 31, page 81). This is called duo-gong after its two main elements: the rectangular block at the top of the column (duo) and the curved cross bar (gong) supporting the beam. This usually carries additional blocks (sheng) on which the beam rests. By the time of the Tang relief, the width of the duo provided the module (cai) for the standardisation of measurements throughout: Tang builders used eight sets of ratios graded in accordance with the hierarchy of building uses – and the rank of the patron.

The hipped roof with its slight curve, shown in the Xi'an relief as at Yungang nearly 200 years earlier not yet in Han reliefs, is typical for the main hall of surviving temples and palaces – lesser halls had gabled ends or gables rising from half-hips, greater later ones had double hips. The tent-like form (see 3, pages 18-19) followed from the flexible structure of superimposed beams, diminishing in length and separated by vertical struts, which supported the purlins, rafters and tiles. As the main elements were stepped horizontals, not diagonals, the structure could readily be extended not only in length but also in width and height – as with the pagoda. The curved roofs were primarily aesthetic but they assisted in throwing water clear of the timbers. The scale of the roof relative to the other two parts of the building was to become much greater in later eras. The apex finials (chiwei) here were fish tails, later dragons, and the plants rising from the ridges were supplemented by animate creatures symbolising water – and as protection against fire.

Under the Tang, temple builders – like the ruling classes – were allowed to elaborate their roofs to achieve daringly cantilevered eaves. Providing shade in the summer but allowing light to enter from the lower sun in the winter, these protected the structure and increased the amount of covered space. Counter-balanced by the main roof structure, the eaves depended on brackets superimposed at right angles to each other to transmit the load of the projecting beam ends bearing the outer purlins. Multiplied with the width of eave overhang, typically the duogong is reiterated to distribute the load over all points of support and, ultimately, between them.

The elaboration of the duogong into identified formulae is the key to the definition of the building – its Order named after the particular bracket formula adopted for it. Structure and decoration were integral in the system but multiplication was to lead to decorative elaboration and, ultimately, to loss of structural significance. The process began with the introduction of smaller intermediate clusters, borne by the beams, continued with the assimilation of these secondary clusters to the primary ones, borne by the columns, went on to the interpolation of still more, the extension of some on the diagonal and their reduction in scale. Indeed, the degree to which decorative elaboration departed from structural necessity distinguishes the eras of later Chinese architectural development.

Early northern temples

The oldest surviving timber buildings in China, of the type represented in the Dacien si relief (see 37, page 92), are found in Shanxi at Wutai shan – the northern Buddhist holy mountain. The small main hall of the Nanchan si (Southern Meditation Temple) dates from 782,[38-39] and the grander great hall of the nearby Foguang si (Temple of the Buddha's Glory) – with its back to the east, exceptionally, in accordance with the nature of its site – was built about 70 years later.[40-44]

Like the one in the relief, these pavilions have three distinct elements: podium, columned structure and pitched roof. The base, which protects the timber structure from damp, was neither exaggerated nor elaborated – as it was later to be – but its height was graded in accordance with the importance of the hall and the need to counteract the size of the roof visually. If not yet quite as overwhelming as it was to become, the roof is already the dominant element in these works and appears both in the hipped and hip-and-gable forms even over a main hall. In the central zone there was always an odd number of bays (jian) defined by posts and partitioned by screens. In the earliest examples, of three and five bays, the timber tra-

38 **Wutai shan, Nanchan si, main hall.**

The main elements of the compound are aligned
north–south. The gatehouse leads to a sunken court flanked
by pavilions of unequal extent and overlooked by a terrace
also flanked by disparate pavilions. The main hall, on the
highest level, is of the type represented in the Xi'an Dacien si
relief except for its half-hipped roof. It has only three bays
to each side, the central ones wider, and no internal

39 **Wutai shan, Nanchan si, main hall, eaves.**
The deep eaves are supported by triple duogong clusters
supported by the columns – there are no intermediate ones
carried on the beams.

columns. The central podium supports a seated image of the
Buddha attended by 16 other figures, including the
bodhisattva Manjusri (Giver of Wisdom).

beated system is fully developed with all the parts both strictly functional and decorative in effect.

Apart from a section revealing the roof structure, the main dimension missing from the relief was colour. Temple roofs were normally of blue-glazed tiles, like the Foguang si, but if a shrine was endowed by a prince or an emperor it may have the distinction of green or yellow roofs like those of noble mansions and imperial palaces respectively. It may be assumed that the columns were protected by coats of lacquer and dyed black with iron sulphate or red with cinnabar – as they are in the Foguang si, and in many later temples and

40 **Wutai shan, Foguang si** longitudinal section and plan.

Founded in 471, the complex was destroyed in the mid-9th-century suppression of the monasteries and begun again almost immediately. The main hall was completed in 857.

The gatehouse to the west leads to a sunken court, as in the Nanchan si (see 38–39, pages 98–99), but there is one large, gable-ended hall dedicated to Manjusri (1115) to the north and several small pavilions to the south. Ascending terraces, the lower one flanked by matching pavilions, culminate in the podium of the Eastern Great Hall – 36 by 20 metres (120 by 65 feet) – and dated to 857 by an inscription on a beam.

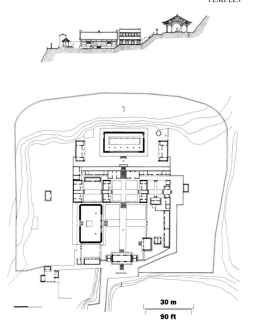

30 m

90 ft

41 **Wutai shan, Foguang si** view from the gatehouse to
the Eastern Great Hall with Manjusri hall (left) and sutra
column (centre).

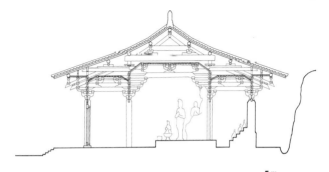

42 **Wutai shan, Foguang si, Eastern Great Hall** lateral section.

43 OVERLEAF **Wutai shan, Foguang si, Eastern Great Hall with founder's tomb (centre)**.

There are seven by four near-square bays to the main hall: the five central ones (slightly wider than the end ones) are screened on the west front, the rest are walled in whole or part. There are two full rows of internal columns, and intermediate columns only between the outer pairs to each side of the image platform that covers slightly more than half the inner area. The deep eaves of the monumental roof – projecting to 4.2 metres (14 feet) – are carried on purlins supported by doubled diagonal beams (ang) which, butting into and counterbalanced by doubled horizontal ones also supporting purlins, penetrate four tiers of duogong over each column. Three-tiered intermediate duogongs resting on the main longitudinal beams carry secondary longitudinal beams. Coffered ceilings are suspended at different levels over the inner and outer zones.

In the centre of the lower court and before the steps of the main hall's podium are octagonal pillars inscribed with sutras between a lotiform base and a tessellated canopy capital: the upper one at least, erected at the same time as the main hall, is the earliest-identified survivor of a type devised to assert the faith.

At the back of the site, to the right of the main hall's podium, is the tomb of the temple's founding abbot. Belonging to the type represented by the Sui stone shrine (see 29, page 74), it is hexagonal, of plastered brick, and embellished with imitation Chinese trabeation and the ogee arch of the Gangetic vernacular.

palaces. The beams, too, were doubtless picked out in multicoloured patterns, as shown even as early as the Yungang shrines (see 31–32, pages 81–83). Walls vary in substance, texture and colour, but if painted they are usually red. The podium was originally undecorated but it was elaborated in form and relief with time, and the greater elevation of the roof.

Even after the Tang persecution of the Buddhists was relaxed in the second half of the 9th century, remains are sparse until the Ming, when temples were built or rebuilt in great numbers. The 10th century is represented by the Longxing si (Temple to the Dragon's Prosperity) at Zhengding, built under the Song from 971, and the Dule si (Temple to Pleasurable Solitude) of Jixian, built under the Liao from 984:[45-48] both are distinguished by multi-storey timber halls sheltering colossal statues of Guanyin. A Tang precedent for this in the Guanyin hall of the Jin'ge si (Golden Tower Temple)[49] on the Wutai shan seems to have been amplified in Ming rebuilding. The main hall of the Jin si (Jin Temple, 1023) at Taiyuan, rising over a complete verandah for perhaps the first

44 Wutai shan, Foguang si, Eastern Great Hall interior.

45 **Jixian, Dule si, gatehouse.**

The gatehouse is hip-roofed over three bays, like the Nanchan si at Wutai Shan (see 38–39, pages 98–99), but is only two bays deep and divided longitudinally by a full row of internal columns to provide a central barrier. The twin bays flanking the outer portico house the guardians that invariably introduce the company of sacred images in Chinese temples.

46 **Jixian, Dule si, gatehouse** interior with guardian.

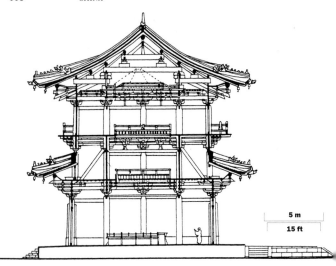

5 m

15 ft

47 **Jixian, Dule si, Guanyin ge** lateral section.

The rectangular main hall, built to house a 16-metre (50-foot) high image of Guanyin, has five bays by four on three floors – or, rather, three tiers of outer and inner colonnades give a triple-height space rising through two galleries. The upper galleries return across the corners to form an octagon, which is echoed by the central conical canopy but not by the coffered ceiling. Outside, the second level of columns is masked by eaves protecting the lower ones, as the main roof overhang protects the upper ones, and a balcony projects from the second gallery level. There is a wide variety of bracket clusters. The purlins of the lower eaves are carried on a four-tier duogong over each of the outer base columns and three-tier intermediate ones. The purlins of the upper eaves are carried on projecting horizontal and diagonal beams supported by a two-tier duogong. The balcony is carried on nearly uniform brackets. To counterbalance the structure, the outer columns of both upper levels are superimposed on a plane slightly inset from those below.

The dedication stele of 986 records a 'restoration' of the temple. As the detail, especially on the gatehouse (see 45–46, pages 108–109), resembles surviving Tang work, it is presumed that the main block follows (even incorporates) a Tang prototype.

48 **Jixian, Dule si, Guanyin ge.**

49 **Wutai shan, Jin'ge si, Guanyin ge**, interior.
Referred to by the Japanese pilgrim Ennin, who visited Buddhist holy sites in China between 838 and 847, the temple was founded in 770 and the two-storey hall roofed in gilded bronze on the order of the Tang Taizong emperor (766–78). It has been rebuilt or restored subsequently, most recently in the mid-1980s.

time on this scale, represents the early 11th century.[50-52] And the multi-storey formula was extended in the mid-11th century for the oldest surviving timber pagoda, in the Fogong si (Temple of the Buddha's Glory) at Yingxian.[53-54]

The elements and their distribution

The earliest surviving temples of the 8th and 9th centuries may not have been strictly formal, but Chinese temples were characteristically symmetrical in their distribution about the longitudinal axis from as early as the 5th century, in the capital of the Northern Wei in fact – as in the Tang Dacien si at Xi'an, and the Song or Liao examples at Jixian, Taiyuan and Yingxian. Generally aligned north–south on an essentially spiritual axis, a series of courts is usually dominated by south-facing pavilions dedicated to manifestations of the deity, ranged hierarchically. Often preceded by a peifang, an entrance screen defining the boundary between the sacred and the profane (see 50, page 117), the entrance is labelled with a calligraphic panel (like all Chinese buildings) and is usually guarded by the fierce warriors Heng and Ha who must be passed before the worshipper is admitted to the first court. Here is the stele pavilion recording the dedication and foundation of the temple, flanked by twin towers for the bell and drum which signal the stations of the devotional day.

Beyond, usually to the north, is the first building of the main sequence, the Tianwang dian, the Hall of the Four Heavenly Kings who rule the quarters of the universe and protect the three jewels of Buddhism: the Buddha, the law and the order of the faithful. These are often represented by an image of the Buddha as Maitreya (lord of the future) flanked by the kings, as the deity is central to the universe. There may be other gates, courts and halls, but the climax in size and position is the Daxiongbao dian (Treasure Hall of the Great Hero) enshrining the main icon of the Buddha – perhaps Guanyin, often Sakyamuni flanked by his youngest and oldest disciples Ananda and Kasyapa, compiler of the scripture and custodian of the tradition respectively.

Structure and decoration
Scaled to the size and import of each hall, the roof is now clearly the dominant element. The Guanyin ge at Yingxian has the gabled roof usually reserved for the

less-important halls flanking courts. So too does the Guanyin ge at Jixian (see 48, page 112), but that was usual for multi-storey buildings, while the gatehouse has a hipped roof (see 45, page 108). Not dedicated to the Buddha but consistent in form with Buddhist sanctuaries, the Shengmu dian in the Taiyuan Jin si (see 51, page 119) has the half-hipped roof that was the norm for multi-tiered forms.

The columns of the Shengmu dian's open east front have dragons curling around their tops in accordance with a 12th-century treatise *Ying zao fa shi* (*Building Methods and Styles*). More significantly, this recommends a standardised duogong and one cluster over each intercolumniate beam except in the case of wider central bays (which need two): here there is one in each bay and they are all similar in size to the ones over the columns. So too with the contemporary Bojiajiaozang dian (Library Hall, 1038) of the Lower Huayan si (Temple of the Huayan Sect) at Datong.[55] This has the half-hipped roof appropriate for a subsidiary building. Inside, sutra cases lend invaluable substance to knowledge of the secular tradition.[56–57]

A century later, decorative play is apparent in the radial disposition of the brackets in Jin works like the

50 Taiyuan, Jin si, entrance screen to main precinct with drum tower and Xi'an dian (Hall of Offerings, centre) early and mid-11th century.

Dedicated to the semilegendary Prince Shuyu, founder of the Jin, which included the Taiyuan area, the temple is first mentioned in literature from the period of the Northern Wei. The area was devastated c. 980 when the Song were attempting to consolidate their hold, but the temple was refounded in the early 11th century when the worship of

Shuyu's mother began to eclipse that of the prince.

Orientated to face the rising sun, the main axis culminates in the earliest surviving works. Beyond the Ming gate (an earlier gate is off-axis to the north) is a Ming stage for the performance of festival plays, Shuijing tai (Water-mirror Platform); beyond is a bridge over the stream that flows through the compound; then a platform with much-recast Song figures in iron; then the three-by-two bay Xi'an dian (rebuilt 1168); then a spring-fed square tank spanned by the cross-shaped Fei liang (Flying Bridge), which was apparently built in place of a Wei predecessor at the same time as the main temple hall immediately to its east, the Shengmu dian (Hall of the Holy Mother, 1023–34, restored under the Yuan and Ming in sympathy with the original).

Of seven by five bays, this has one of the earliest examples of a two-tier, half-hipped roof – the lower tier covering a verandah ambulatory consistent in detail with the main structure (and 11th-century work elsewhere). Though the similarity of the principal and secondary duogong approaches the Song norm, Song consistency is not achieved in detail. For example, some of the diagonal beams still butt up against horizontal beams, some support purlins at both ends. The two inner rows of columns are deleted to house the Song icons of the holy mother and her retinue.

51 **Taiyuan, Jin si, Shengmu dian (Hall of the Holy Mother), east front** 1023–34.

52 **Taiyuan, Jin si, Shengmu dian** detail of verandah with guardian.

53 **Yingxian, Fogong si, pagoda.**

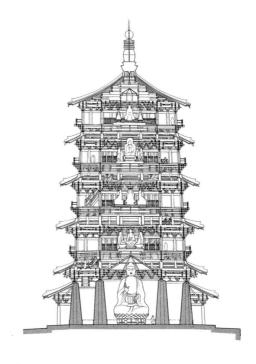

54 **Yingxian, Fogong si, pagoda** section.

The pagoda, built from 1056 in the centre of the complex, is an octagon 30 metres (100 feet) at base that rises through five storeys (each with a blind mezzanine and central shrine) to over 67 metres (220 feet). Like the timber Guanyin ge at the Dule si in Jixian (see 47–48, pages 110–112), but unlike the typical masonry pagoda with its load-bearing walls and central piers or stairs, the structure depends on two concentric rings of columns at each level. Here, however, each of the tiers is stepped back from the one below like the sections of a ship's mast – hence the storeys diminish progressively to both structural and aesthetic advantage. The ground floor is embraced by a veranda, the upper ones by cantilevered galleries. Flexible joints in the major and minor members of the timber frame throughout have obviated destruction by earthquake.

55 Datong, Huayan si, Bojiajiaozang dian (Library Hall), lower compound 1038.

The complex is orientated to the east, reputedly in accordance with the devotion of its original Liao patrons to the sun. Burned during the sack of Datong at the end of the Liao dynasty (1122), the temple was rebuilt by the Jin in its two present compounds, extended by the Ming and largely rebuilt by the Qing. The Library Hall in the lower compound is the sole survivor from the Liao period, the main hall of the upper compound is the sole survivor of the Jin period.

Five bays by four, enshrining 31 icons, the Library Hall's back and side walls are lined with 38 sutra stacks in the form of the Palace of the Western Paradise. Most notable is the central hall on a bridge connecting it to side pavilions. The earliest-surviving three-dimensional representation of a Chinese palace, presumably a reduction of the Liao one adapted to the special requirements of the library, its resemblance to the Tang Han-yuan dian (see 13, page 43) is striking. In the models, as on the exterior of the library itself, bracketing approaches mature Song *gravitas*.

56 **Datong, Huayan si, Bojiajiaozang dian** interior.

57 **Datong, Huayan si, Bojiajiaozang dian** detail of sutra cases in the form of a model palace.

58 PREVIOUS PAGES **Datong, Shanhua si** 1128.

Founded under the Tang in c. 740 and partly destroyed in the sack of Datong, the temple was restored by the Jin between 1123 and 1143, and again under the mid-15th-century Ming. The gatehouse with Ming guardians and the first prayer hall, Sansheng dian, with Jin figures of the Buddha flanked by the bodhisattvas Manjusri (Wisdom) and Samantabhadra (Benevolence), seem to have been rebuilt from 1123.

The main hall, of seven bays by five (with Liao icons), seems to have been restored from 1123: it provides the immediate precedent in monumentality for the Daxiongbao dian of Datong's Upper Huayan si. The Puxian Gate (Samantabhadra pavilion, inserted in 1154 towards the centre of the western wall of the compound) belongs to the type of multi-storey building represented by the Tayuan si library (see 70, page 145) and the Guanyin ge of the Jin'ge si on Wutai shan (see 49, page 113), evidently Tang in origin but rebuilt under the Ming, as well as the late 10th-century Dule si at Jixian (see 47–48, pages 110–112).

59 **Datong, Shanhua si, Sansheng dian.**
Note the radial disposition of the intermediate brackets.

60 **Datong, Shanhua si, Sansheng dian** interior.

61 Datong, Huayan si, Daxiongbao dian (Powerful Treasure Hall of the Great Hero), upper compound 1140, interior.

Nine bays by five on a platform 4.5 metres (15 feet) high, this is the largest surviving hall from before the Ming era, when there was a proliferation of the double-eave roof. To house the huge Buddhas (1427) there are two, not four, rows of internal columns inset from the ambulatory duogong.

Sansheng dian (Hall of the Three Sages) of the Shanhua si (Temple of the Great Transformation) at
Datong.[58-60] However, the main building there and
the Upper Huayan si, both with vast hipped roofs,
show a weighty consistency of bracketing which
approaches the Song ideal both in the assimilation of
the primary and secondary clusters, and in the shape
and scale of the parts.[61] Further, these buildings
exhibit a new *gravitas* in the revision of the ratio
between column and roof height which anticipated the
monumentality of the Ming without resorting to the
doubling of the eaves.

Southern variants

In the hot and humid south of the country ventilation
was a major concern of builders. The upward-curv-
ing corners of eaves, left open between the duogong,
were clearly devised to catch the air – but the flair
with which they did so was equally southern in its
appeal. Thus, elegant in line rather than severely
monumental in their mass, the southern temples were
nonetheless rigorously axial in distribution than their
northern counterparts – unlike the capitals of the
Southern Song.

62 **Suzhou, Baoen si, Beisi (Northern Temple Pagoda)**

mid-12th century, restored late 19th century.

The pagoda rises through nine storeys of brick and timber to a height of 76 metres (250 feet).

The most prominent Song foundations in Hangzhou were destroyed with much of the city during the Taiping rebellion (1860–62). In Suzhou, however, the Baoen si (Temple of Gratitude), with its impressive pagoda, survives in its southern Song form – if much restored.[62–63] Further south, in Fuzhou and Xiamen respectively, the Yongquan si (Temple of the Gushing Spring)[64] and Nanputuo si (Southern Temple of the Putuo Sect)[65–67] well represent southern style: the latter has the fluidity and floridity of a late epoch, but the main hall of the former, at least, retains its Song character despite later imperial patronage.

Later religious buildings

Lamaists and their virulent Muslim opponents, Confucianists and Daoists, all adapted the traditional

63 **Suzhou, Baoen si from the Beisi pagoda.**
 Reputedly founded by a mid-3rd-century ruler of Wu, the temple was destroyed in conflict between the Song and Jin in 1130 and rebuilt under the Shaoxing emperor (1131–63). The pagoda provides the focus for the celebrated 'borrowed view' from the Zhuozheng yuan (Garden of the Humble Administrator) (see 110, pages 210–211).

64 **Fuzhou, Yongquan si, Tianwang dian (Hall of the Heavenly Kings).**

The temple was founded in 908 but the scale of the three main halls aligned on the principal axis (the Tianwang dian is nearest the spring) suggests a Song date at the earliest. Like the rest of the complex it was restored many times – especially under the Qing Kangxi (1662–1722) and Qianlong (1736–96) emperors who favoured it. The twin ceramic pagodas of the court (inscribed in 1082, moved from the Longrui si in 1972) are typical of the Southern Song in their elaborate representation of a multi-storey structure.

65 **Xiamen, Nanputuo si** outer court with Qin dian
(enshrining Maitreya accompanied by the four heavenly
kings, right), twin pagodas in the southern tradition and
bell tower (left), date unknown.

67 **Xiamen, Nanputuo si, Daxiong bodian (Precious Hall of the Great Hero)** interior with the Buddhas Shakyamuni, Yaoshi and Amitabha.

66 **Xiamen, Nanputuo si, Dabai dian** enshrining a statue of Guanyin.

Chinese columned hall to their purposes after the pattern set by the early Buddhists. The Lamaseries in Wutai shan[68-70] and Beijing,[71] the Qingzhen si (Great Mosque) at Xi'an,[72-75] the Temple of Confucius in Beijing,[76] and the Daoist Chunyang gong (Temple of the Purity of the Yang) in Taiyuan[77] may be taken as representative. Quite exceptional is the Xuangong si (Suspended Temple) of Hongyuan,[78-79] a Daoist foundation dedicated to accord with Buddhism and Confucianism in a unique syncretism. Dedicated to the supreme expression of Confucianism, but reflecting celestial and terrestrial symbolism in its form is the Tian tan (Temple of Heaven) in Beijing[82-85] where the emperor went each year at the winter solstice to render an account of his stewardship over the past year and to be associated with the imperial ancestors in the invocation of heaven's favour for the year to come. Its

68 Wutai shan, Xiantong monastery (Manifest Penetration) compound.

The monastery was reputedly founded in the mid-1st century AD. It has been reconstructed many times and is now substantially Ming – as the interpolated decoration fringing the beams and column tops indicates here.

69 Wutai shan, Xiantong and Tayuan si (Dagoba Temple) monasteries, Tayuan dagoba and double-height sutra library (left).

Wutai shan is dedicated to the bodhisattva Manjusri who is believed to have alighted there. As Manjusri is of special significance to the Lamaist Buddhism of Tibet and Mongolia, the holy mountain is a place of pilgrimage: hence the Tibetan bulbous form of dagoba, probably Yuan in origin but restored under the Ming Hongwu emperor (1368–98) when its compound, originally part of Xiantong, was given its separate identity.

70 **Wutai shan, Tayuan si, library** interior with sutra case.

The 20-tier, hexagonal sutra case was noted by the Japanese pilgrim Ennin in the Tang era. Presumably then, as now, it rose through a double-height space. Ming work on the building has subsequently been restored several times. The device of the revolving sutra case, ascribed to a mid-6th-century monk, was deployed many times. There is another prominent example in the Longxing si at Zhengding.

special combination of square and circular elements symbolises the conjunction of heaven and earth.

These buildings may be taken as representative of the Ming and Qing eras along with those of the Buddhists, who remained the greatest patrons – or recipients of imperial patronage – under both of these dynasties.[80–81] In general, these eras saw the amplification and elaboration of form, especially in multi-

71 Beijing, Yonghe gong (Palace of Harmony converted to Lamaism) late 17th century.

The palace built for the fourth son of the Qing Kangxi emperor was converted to an imperial ancestral gallery on his unexpected accession to the throne as the Yongzheng emperor (1723–35) – as it was contrary to propriety for an imperial residence to be inhabited by anyone else – and assigned to Tibetan lamas in 1744 by the Qianlong emperor with whom Lamaism found special favour. There are five courts: the Chaotian men (Gate of Shining Glory) leads to the outer court, with bell and drum towers, and stele pavilions, before the Tianwang dian (with Maitreya flanked by the four heavenly kings) whose south-facing façade is blind except for the central three arcaded bays. The second court precedes the Taihe dian (Hall of Supreme Harmony) with the past, present and future Buddhas. The third court is preceded by the Yongyou dian (Hall of Eternal Protection with the Buddhas of medicine and longevity) and precedes the stupa-roofed Falun dian (Hall of the Wheel of the Law with a statue of Tsongkhapa, the founder of the Geluk order of Tibetan Lamaism that produced the line of the Dalai Lamas). The axial sequence (flanked by many other buildings) culminates in the three-storey Wanfu ge (Pavilion of Ten-thousand Happinesses housing an 18-metre/59-foot high image of Maitreya) linked by bridges to side pavilions (for ordination and special guests). This recalls the form of palace represented in the Lower Huayan si at Datong (see 59, page 131) and, beyond that, by the Han-yuan dian of Tang Chang'an (see 13, page 43).

72 **Xi'an, Qingzhen si** plan.

(1) Outer court and timber screen; (2) stele court with stone screen; (3) octagonal minaret; (4) inner court with fountain and ablution tank; (5) prayer hall and terrace; (6) school for teaching Islam (madrasa); (7) bath house and accommodation for pilgrims.

Founded in 742, the present form dates from the early 16th century, but the complex was restored in the early 17th

20 m
60 ft

and late 18th centuries, and (thoroughly) in the 1980s. As always with mosques east of Mecca, it is orientated with the wall sealing the prayer hall to the west indicating the direction of prayer.

Built almost entirely in accordance with the Chinese trabeated tradition, like the main mosque of Beijing but unlike most of the many mosques which line the Silk Road through Xinjiang, it is now entered from the north. The first (eastern) courtyard is dominated by the timber screen. The main gate, on the principal axis, leads to a stele with a stone screen. Beyond is a second gate leading to the court of the octagonal minaret, flanked by the lecture hall and residential cells of the madrasa. Triple stone portals lead to the inner court with fountain and ablution tank, flanked by a bath house and a accommodation for pilgrims. From this steps lead through a second set of triple portals to a prayer platform immediately before the seven-bay prayer hall.

73 **Xi'an, Qingzhen si, octagonal minaret.**

74 **Xi'an, Qingzhen si, fountain court.**

75 **Xi'an, Qingzhen si, main prayer hall.**

76 Beijing, Temple of Confucius.

First built in the Yuan period (1279–1368) to house the ancestral tablets of Confucius, this was the scene of special ceremonies attended by the emperor on the birthday of the sage. The present buildings are Ming and Qing.

77 Taiyuan, Chunyang gong view from a simulated mountain.

The Daoists used 'gong' (palace) for their temples rather than the Buddhist 'si'. Now part of the provincial museum, the temple was a mansion dedicated under the Ming Wanli emperor (1573–1619) to Lu Dongbin, a semi-legendary Daoist sage. Beyond the three-bay Lu dian (Hall of the Daoist Immortal Lu), adapted from the main hall of the house, it was extended under the Qing Qianlong emperor (1736–96) to the inner courts with the three-storey pavilion and its satellites.

Daoists habitually sought secluded sites amid nature of exceptional beauty or particular difficulty – areas that are not urban, by definition. Thus, where a great master was to be honoured in the place of his urban existence, the ideal was to be simulated. Contrary to the axial norm, a mountain of contorted rocks was raised to the side of an extended forecourt before the main gate to the original mansion, and a great deal of rockery was distributed throughout the inner courts.

78 **Hongyuan, Xuangong si.**
Founded under the Northern Wei in the early 6th century, the so-called suspended monastery's site could hardly better represent the Daoist ideal. The present buildings are Ming and Qing. The syncretic shrine is the top-most one.

79 **Hongyuan, Xuangong si, syncretic shrine** the Buddha flanked by Confucius and Laozi.

80 **Taiyuan, Chongshan si (Temple of the Veneration of Goodness), Guanyin ge.**
Refounded in 1381 on a Song base, the monastery was largely destroyed by fire in 1865, but the hall survived: the Boddhisattva of Mercy is flanked by a Manjusri to her right and Samantabhadra to her left.

81 **Taiyuan, Chongshan si, Guanyin ge** interior.

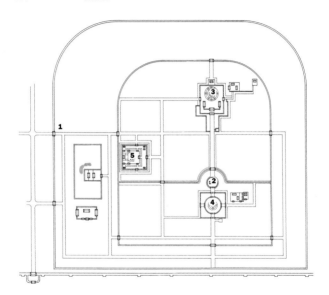

82 **Beijing, Tian tan** plan.

(1) Imperial entrance; (2) Huangqiong yu (Vault of Imperial Heaven); (3) Qinian dian (Hall of Prayer for Good Harvests); (4) Huangqiu (Altar of Heaven); (5) Zhai gong (Palace of Abstinence).

Founded in 1420 as the Temple of Heaven and Earth but assigned exclusively to Heaven after the Ming Jiajing emperor (1522–66) constructed separate sanctuaries for the Sun, Moon and Earth, the double compound is rectangular to the south (in accordance with the ancient Chinese conception of the earth as square) and circular to the north (symbolising heaven). It is entered from the west by the emperor but otherwise from the north, in accordance with Zhou prescription that the Tian tan should be to the south of a city. In agreement with the invariable ritual to be performed there, the complex is rigorously axial in the alignment of its principal elements. Circular in accordance with their heavenly dedication these are: the three-storey Qinian dian (1420, restored in the mid-18th and late 19th centuries), the two-storey Huangqiong yu, and the unroofed three-tiered platform of the Huangqiu on its square (earthly) base. To the west, between two gates, is the Zhai gong which, representing the earthly abode of the son of heaven, is rectangular.

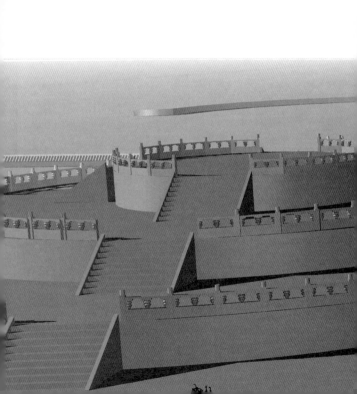

storey buildings and with a special debt to the Tibetan tradition. In particular, they are distinguished by the degree to which the elaboration of the bracket system departed from structural necessity. This has already been apparent in the comparison of the survivors of the Tang period at Wutai shan (see 38 and 42, pages 98 and 103) with the Song pavilions at the Taiyuan Jin si (see 50, page 117) and, further, the Jin buildings of Datong (see 55 and 58, pages 125 and 128–129). Now the repetition of the accumulated duogong provides a continuous frieze that seems to separate, rather than to connect,

83 PREVIOUS PAGES **Beijing, Tian tan** reconstructed view from the Huangqiu.

On the day before the winter solstice, entering by the north-west gate, the emperor went to the Huangqiong yu to honour the tablets of his ancestors kept there. Then he retired to the Zhai gong for a night of meditation and privation. On the solstice day, accompanied by the tablets, the emperor proceeded to the Huangqiu to sacrifice animals and to render an account of the past year directly to heaven. He returned to the Qinian dian (again accompanied by the tablets) in the first month to pray for heaven's favour in good harvests in the coming year.

84 Beijing, Tian tan, Qinian dian.

The Qinian dian – 30 metres (100 feet) in diameter and
37.5 metres (120 feet) high – with storeys clearly
differentiated in width, is not constructed on the principle
of the stepped mast first encountered at the Fogong si at
Yingxian (see 54, page 123): 12 outer columns support the roof
of the lower storey.

the forest of columns rising from the multi-tiered base and the enormous double roof characteristic of all imperial building types after the advent of the Ming.

85 Beijing, Tian tan, Qinian dian interior.

Twelve inner columns support the roof of the second storey, four rising 18 metres (59 feet) from the ground, and eight from circular beams suspended from the main ones at the apex of the lower roof but carried by cross-beams resting on the outer colonnade. The top roof is carried on 12 more, smaller, columns supported on the brackets borne by the ones below and counterbalanced by the eaves – but most of this is concealed by the coffering of the second-storey ceiling. The number of revealed columns relates the building to the heavenly cycle, governing life on earth: the outer 12 represent the months, the inner ones the 12 'hours' into which the day and night were traditionally divided, and the four main ones the seasons.

86 **Jing ling (Scenic Tomb) of the Ming Xuande emperor (reigned 1425–35).**

Tombs in ancient China were tumuli with underground chambers – often simulating houses – for the sarcophagus surrounded by all the treasures and necessities of life to sustain the soul of the deceased throughout eternity (see 5, page 24). As these were places for worshipping ancestors, a succession of pavilions reproducing the halls and courts of the gods – and of man – for offerings, prayer and inhumation ceremonies preceded the mound which protected and commemorated the burial.[86]

By the time of the Ming – indeed probably as early as the Zhou – the court, or courts, containing the halls for living worshippers and earthly obsequies was square whereas the mound representing the eternal abode of the departed son of heaven was circular. And the dictates of *feng shui* were paramount: the prescriptions for harmonising with nature on well-drained ground, facing south and protected by hills to the north may have been practical in origin, but aspiration to rapport with the spirit of the site in the disposition of the tomb attained the transcendental domain of geomancy.

The tomb of the founder of the Ming dynasty, the Hongwu emperor Zhu Yuanzhang (reigned

1368–98), was installed outside his capital, Nanjing.[87] After a pavilion sheltering the stele inscribed with the emperor's titles (and borne by a tortoise, representing longevity), the circuitous path of the spirit way (devised to deter evil spirits who can only travel in straight lines) leads between symbolic beasts to an avenue, lined with civil and military officers, and aligned north–south with the axis of the tomb. Five bridges over a river (*feng shui* requires water at the foot of a site) lead to the square platform that supported the prayer and obsequy halls preceding the circular mound.

Zhu Yuanzhang designated his grandson as his successor but Cheng Zhu, one of his younger sons and governor of Beijing, overthrew his nephew, assumed the throne as the Yongle emperor (reigned 1402–24) and moved the capital back to Beijing in 1402. He and a dozen of his Ming successors were buried in a beautiful south-facing arc of hills at the base of the Tianshou Shan to the north-west of the northern capital.

After a white and red screen, the spirit way begins at a pavilion sheltering the tortoise-borne stele inscribed with the titles of the emperors interred at the site, as at Nanjing. It then leads northwards to the

87 Xiao ling (Filial Tomb) of Zhu Yuanzhang, spirit way.

88 OVERLEAF Chang ling of the Yongle emperor, Ling'en dian (Hall of Offerings).
The main hall of the Chang ling, on the earliest of the imperial three-tiered marble podia and under an awesome two-tiered hip roof, is the precedent for the palace halls of the imperial capital and is only slightly smaller than the largest of them.

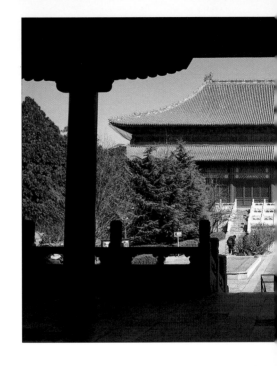

89 **Chang ling of the Yongle emperor, Minglou.**

Chang ling (Long-lasting Tomb) but after the
Longfeng men (Dragon and Phoenix Gate, the dragon
for the emperor, the phoenix for the empress) near the
centre of the site paths diverge to the other parts of the
necropolis. Varied in size, the tombs are consistent in
form. Like Yongle's Chang ling, the grandest have
three courts: a yellow-roofed gate (with three doors,
the central one for the departed emperor, the left one
for his successor) leads to the outer court. A second
gate, the Ling'en men (Gate of Heavenly Favours),
leads to the court and hall of the same designation, in
which the emperor's forebears were honoured and his
own birthday remembered.[88] Another triple gate leads
to the third court with its central altar table bearing
carved replicas of the implements used for the obsequies. Beyond is the towered gatehouse (Minglou,
with the stele of the interred emperor in the upper
chamber)[89] of the circular compound containing the
pine-covered burial mound with its excavated corri-
dors and chambers.

In a setting as beautiful as that of their Ming predecessors, five of the Qing emperors are buried on the
south-facing slopes of the Changrui Shan, east of Beijing. The main tombs are those of the Kangxi emperor

90 Yu ling (Fortunate Tomb) of the Qing Qianlong emperor.

91 Yu ling, tomb chamber.

and his grandson, the Qianlong emperor,[90-91] but the tomb of the notorious Empress Dowager Cixi is notable if only for excess. Approached by a spirit way and beyond a river, they are similar in constitution to the Ming tombs, though there are usually more side pavilions (some to cater for Lamaist prayers) and the base and the Yu ling underground 'palace' is embellished with exceptionally rich reliefs of Buddhist (specifically Lamaist) and imperial symbolism. There are separate tombs for empresses, contrary to usual Ming practice.

Secular works in towns are also invariably complexes of courts and halls aligned strictly north–south, with the back to the north where the wall – as at the back of China – was designed to keep out evil. The authority of the axis over the plan of town, temple, palace and house was essentially Confucian, and the informality of the villa and its garden setting was essentially Daoist – the assertion of control and the recognition of the uncontrollable representing the *yang* and *yin* of wholeness.

The Forbidden City
Few exercises in axial planning have rivalled the Imperial Palace in the so-called Forbidden City in Beijing – since the greatest of the ancient Egyptian temples (see volume 1, ORIGINS, page 127), at least. Begun almost immediately after the Yongle emperor had established his capital on the Yuan site at the beginning of the 15th century, it respected the ancient Zhou ideal honoured by Confucius with a succession of courts and pavilions in two zones and three parallel ranges.[92–93] Beyond the southern gate in the main compound,[94] the yellow roofs of the grandest timber halls the world has seen[95–98] – at least since Persepolis (see volume 3,

92 **Beijing, Forbidden City, Imperial Palace** plan.
(1) Wu men (Meridian Gate to outer zone of the
Forbidden City); (2) Court of Golden Stream and Dragon
Bridge; (3) Taihe men (Gate of Supreme Harmony), flanked
by the Zhaode men and Zhendu men (Gates of Luminous
Virtue and Correct Conduct) to ceremonial zone; (4) Taihe
dian (Hall of Supreme Harmony); (5) Zhonghe dian (Hall
of Perfect Harmony); (6) Baohe dian (Hall of Preserving
Harmony); (7) Qianqing men (Gate of Heavenly Purity) to
private zone; (8) Qianqing gong (Palace of Heavenly Purity);
(9) Jiaotai gong (Palace of Prosperity); (10) Kunning gong
(Palace of Earthly Tranquillity); (11) Kunning men (Gate of
Earthly Tranquillity); (12) Yuhua yuan (Imperial Garden);
(13) Shenwu men (Gate of Martial Spirit); (14) Yangxin
gong (Palace of Mental Cultivation); (15) Ningshou gong
(Palace of Peaceful Longevity).

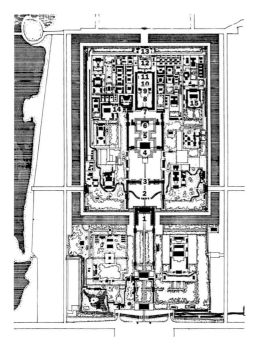

93 Beijing, Forbidden City, Imperial Palace.

In the walled rectangle of the northern sector of Beijing is the Imperial City. Once walled and entered through the great Tianan'men (Gate of Heavenly Peace), originally at the head of a relatively narrow avenue, now addressing the vastness of Red Square, this inner city contained administrative offices, ministerial residences, imperial factories, parks and the palace compound. Still stoutly walled and moated, the palace compound (750 by 960 metres/2460 by 3150 feet) is the innermost nucleus, the Forbidden City, the residence of the emperor and the seat of government – and entry beyond its Wu men was forbidden to all except the imperial family and those on imperial business (who were admitted only to the outer zone).

The Yongle emperor is reputed to have impressed up to 300,000 workers in the construction of his new palace in the new northern capital from 1407. Covering 7.2 square kilometres (3 square miles), it took 14 years to realise the basic conception which greatly exceeds the prescriptions for the palace laid down in the Zhou treatise on imperial planning, *Kao gong ji*. That required a succession of five gates for the increasingly exclusive compounds, a succession of two zones for the public ceremonial and private residence, and a succession of three great halls for the functions of state. In Beijing the two zones embrace five major courts and six major pavilions, one for each function of the imperial life – apart from nearly 9000 subsidiary spaces.

94 **Beijing, Forbidden City, Imperial Palace, Wu men.**

The five-arched Wu men (built by 1417, restored 1647 and 1801) is unique for its massive three-winged base: from the central pavilion imperial proclamations were read and the Qing emperors reviewed troops and prisoners of war. Beyond, the first court of the palace (surrounded by galleries and storerooms) is cut by the Jinshui (Golden Waters) crossed by the Long qiao (Dragon Bridge) – the five bridges represent the Confucian virtues: benevolence, propriety, righteousness, reliability and wisdom. Beyond, guarded by twin lions (non-indigenous but ubiquitous symbols of royal power) is the Taihe men (early 15th century, last rebuilt in the late 19th century) leading to the court of that designation and the three-tiered, elaborately balustraded platform (7 metres/23 feet high) that bears the three pavilions of the outer, ceremonial zone. The central flight of steps is divided by a marble ramp reserved for the passage of the emperor in his palanquin and is, therefore, embellished with his dragon symbol.

95 PREVIOUS PAGES **Beijing, Forbidden City, Taihe dian.**

The first of the ceremonial halls is the 11-bay Taihe dian. At 64 by 37 metres (210 by 120 feet) it is the largest of all the imperial two-tiered, hipped-roof halls; finished in 1417, burned and rebuilt in 1421 and 1557, it has been renovated several times since. It was used for imperial enthronement, to celebrate the imperial birthday, the winter solstice and the new year, for major audiences, and for the issue of major instruments of state. On his screened throne, below the dragon emblazoned on the central canopy of the coffered ceiling, the emperor would be attended by the imperial family and senior administrators within, by the vast army of court and government officials in the great court without. Columns and screen walls are red, the multiple brackets and beams are multicoloured (predominantly green and gold), and the roof tiles are yellow, as propriety requires for imperial buildings. The main roof ridges terminate in dragon acroteria 3.4 metres (11 feet) high, and the diagonal ridges have 12 symbolic creatures (the highest number on any Chinese building).

96 **Beijing, Forbidden City, Taihe dian.**

97 OVERLEAF **Beijing, Forbidden City, Taihe dian**
interior.

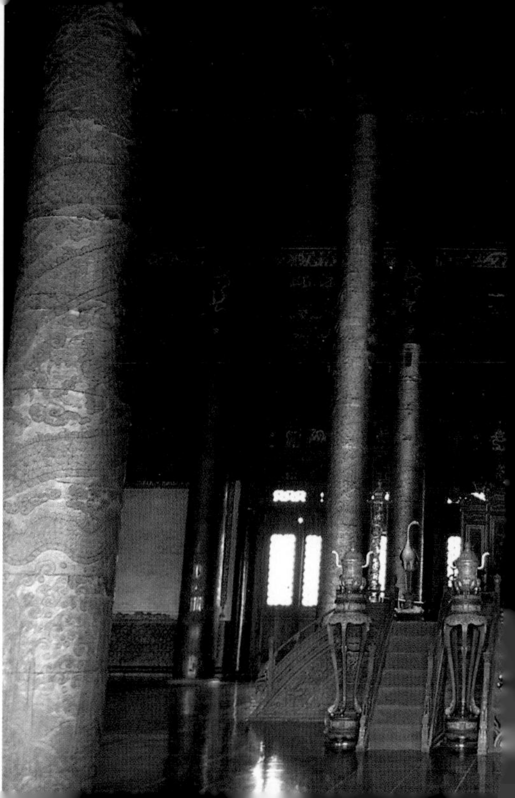

98 Beijing, Forbidden City, Zhonghe dian with Baohe dian (behind).

The Zhonghe dian and Baohe dian that follow the Taihe dian on the triple platform are square and rectangular respectively: the former (with a pyramidal roof) was where the emperor prepared for ceremonies in the main hall; the latter (repeating the formula of the Taihe dian to a reduced scale but with a hip-and-gable roof) was where imperial banquets and triennial examinations for the imperial administrative service were held.

99 Beijing, Forbidden City, pavilions for the emperor's wives and concubines.

Beyond another staircase divided by the largest marble ramp in the whole complex, the outer and inner zones are separated by a court and linked by the Qianqing men, guarded by another pair of lions. On a single terrace and reproducing the outer complex on a smaller scale are the three halls (1417) of the imperial residence. The dragon-embellished Qianqing gong (thrice destroyed before its final rebuilding in 1797) was the emperor's reception hall and bed chamber until the Yongzheng emperor moved out in 1723. It is flanked by the imperial wardrobe, study, secretariat and school room; the square, pyramidal-roofed, phoenix-embellished Jiaotai gong was where the imperial seals were stored and where the empress received homage. The hip-roofed Kunning gong was where the empresses slept and received the emperor (until 1723), and where the esoteric religious rites favoured by Mongols and Manchus were performed. All the pavilions of the complex are divided only in so far as their colonnades form ambulatories or distinguish the central throne area, but the Kunning gong is partitioned into rooms for private purposes.

Beyond the Kunning gong, the gate of the same name leads to the Yuhua yuan that terminates the main axis in the north. To the west of the inner zone is the relatively modest Yangxin gong and its garden, to which the Yongzheng emperor resorted in the 1720s instead of the Qianqing gong. The later Qing emperors lived here too, and their wives and concubines were housed in small palaces to its north. In the corresponding part of the eastern zone are the palaces of the heir apparent and his entourage, and the palace and garden built by the Qianlong emperor for his retirement (1795). In the southern sectors are shrines, service buildings, including a library, a printing press, guard accommodation and an archery ground.

IMPERIAL FORM, page 12) – dominate the outer zone of public ceremonial and government though the residential halls of the emperor and empress in the private inner zone are scarcely less impressive.[99]

The tripartite composition of the pavilions has been amplified on a truly imperial scale with the multi-tiered podia and higher, steeper roofs of the tomb of the Yongle emperor (see 89, page 174): these are less flared in overhang, more rigid in line, less dynamic, more crushingly monumental than anything encountered before. Imperial too in their sumptuousness, the structures that support the roofs have been elaborated – especially with the repetition of bracket clusters unsupported by posts – to the point where richness obscures function.

Town houses

Down the social scale, housing conformed to the courtyard type wherever the Han penetrated in China: in a walled compound court succeeds court, with the number of pavilions aligned on axis responding to the social status and economic resources of the extended family – usually parents, unmarried children, married sons, additional wives, spinsters and servants.[100-101]

100 Beijing, courtyard housing north-west of the Imperial City.

Extra buildings were inserted in the courtyards when this type of house was assigned to multi-family occupation on the advent of Communism.

101 Beijing, typical two-courtyard house plan.
(1) Entrance; (2) ante-space before; (3) inner door; (4) first (reception) court; (5) main hall; (6) service courts.

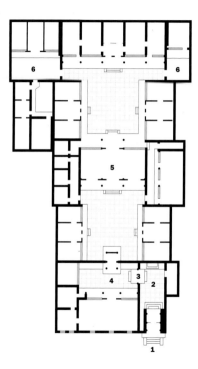

The nature of the form is introverted, with light, air, circulation and reception space provided by the court, but *feng shui* dictates a north–south axis: walled from the evil of the north, the trabeated structure of the main pavilions is open to the sun and all the good of the south.

Typically, as with the ancient Roman house (see volume 3, IMPERIAL FORM, page 165), the door to the first main space is on axis, but as with the ancient Greek house (see volume 3, IMPERIAL FORM, page 68) the street entrance is usually to the side of the virtually blind outer wall.[102] In Beijing, typically, it faces the blind masonry enclosing an ante-space before the axial inner door to preserve the privacy of the interior from the view of passers-by – and to prevent the entry of evil spirits. Not invariable, especially in the south, this is contrary to the norm for temples and palaces, where entrance to the public zone (at least) is on axis, but the portal of the grandest houses is preceded by a screen – as before a temple (see 50, page 117) or palace. The main south-facing pavilion not only houses the tablets of the ancestors and the altar of the family's patron deity, like the Roman tablinum, but also it accommodates the senior males.[103] The side pavilions of the simplest

102 **Beijing, courtyard house, street entrance.**

103 **Beijing, courtyard house, outer court.**

104 **Beijing, courtyard house, service court.**

105 **Suzhou, block housing in a district by the Beisi pagoda** (see 62, page 135).

houses are for male servants as well as junior members of the family, the inner courts of the richer ones are for the female members of the family and children, and the rear courts are for retainers, female servants, kitchens, laundries, baths, etc.[104]

As in ancient Rome, the density of urban development often prompted the integration of shops, contraction of the court and addition of storeys – especially in the south and beyond in south-east Asia, to which the Chinese exported their traditions, where ventilation was needed more than exposure to sun and rain. In the south, in fact, other types were developed – or inherited from pre-Han inhabitants: in particular, rooms were doubled and superimposed in compact blocks addressing the street in front and a yard behind.[105] Naturally, these depended on stout masonry walls rather than trabeation, though outer walls were generally thinner in the humid south; larger spaces required inner columns, and roofs were supported by the superimposed beams of the Chinese norm.

Responding to the way of the Daoists back to nature – away from the *yang* of the town, back to the *yin* of the wild – the gardens of China are essentially private evocations of the landscape at large, taking advantage of natural topography where possible, simulating it where necessary no matter what the scale. Like the paintings and poems that inspire them, their characteristics include variety, irregularity, asymmetry, mystery and originality. Their elements are natural and man-made: earth and rock, water and plants, architecture and sculpture. Indeed, the integration of the natural and artificial is the major achievement of the Chinese gardener, his prime objective being complete harmony with the spirit of the wilderness for passive contemplation of the relationship between man and nature – not least his own.[106–114]

Usually attached to a suburban or country house, sometimes to a particularly grand town mansion, architecture defined the context and provided the accommodation in the garden: walls enclose the site

106 **Wuxi, Jichang yuan (Garden of the Love of Attachment), entrance** early 16th century on a Yuan foundation.

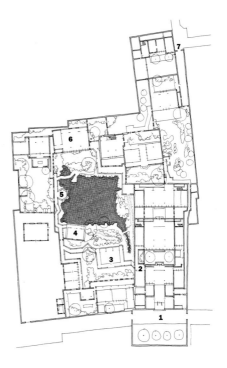

107 **Suzhou, Wangshi yuan (Garden of the Master of the Nets)** early 13th century and restored in the late 19th century, plan.

(1) Entrance to courtyard house; (2) entrance to garden; (3) Xiaoshanconggui ting (Hall of Small Mountains and Osmanthus Spring), main garden reception gallery; (4) Zhuoying ting (Pavilion for Contemplating the Water); (5) Yuedaofenglai xia (Gazebo for Catching the Breeze and Contemplating the Moon); (6) Kansongduhua ting (Verandah for Gazing at the Pines and Studying Paintings), retreat for study; (7) rear entrance.

Though seclusion was the prime objective of the Chinese gardener, in practice he was not generally a complete recluse in town or suburban gardens like those of Suzhou. There, planning usually started with the placing of the main reception pavilion (ting), usually open (or at least fenestrated) to all sides and normally to the south of the main body of water. The other garden building types, the gazebo (xia or xuan) for contemplating a view or a particular feature of the garden and the retreat for study in the most secluded part, follow the disposition of the natural elements – real or contrived.

108 **Suzhou, Wangshi yuan** view from the west wall of
the house over the 'lake' to the Yuedaofenglai ting and
verandah.

109 **Suzhou, Zhuozheng yuan (Garden of the Humble Administrator), Yuanxiang ting (Hall of Distant Fragrance)** interior.

110 OVERLEAF **Suzhou, Zhuozheng yuan** view east through the middle zone to the Wuzhuyouju ting (Retreat Among the Bamboos and Parasol Trees).

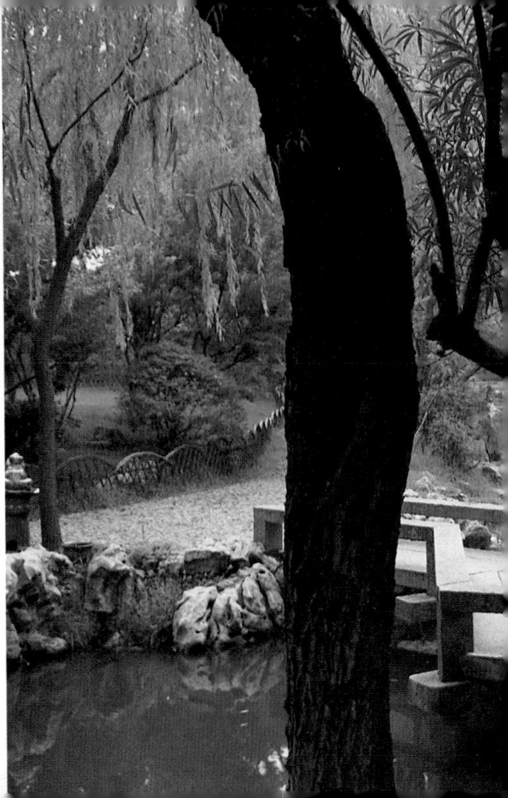

111 **Suzhou, Zhuozheng yuan** view west through the moon-gate between the two zones.

112 **Shanghai, Yu yuan (Garden of Content)** window framing a 'living picture' and an internal 'borrowed view'.

113 OVERLEAF **Shanghai, Yu yuan** 1560s, moon-gate between courts.

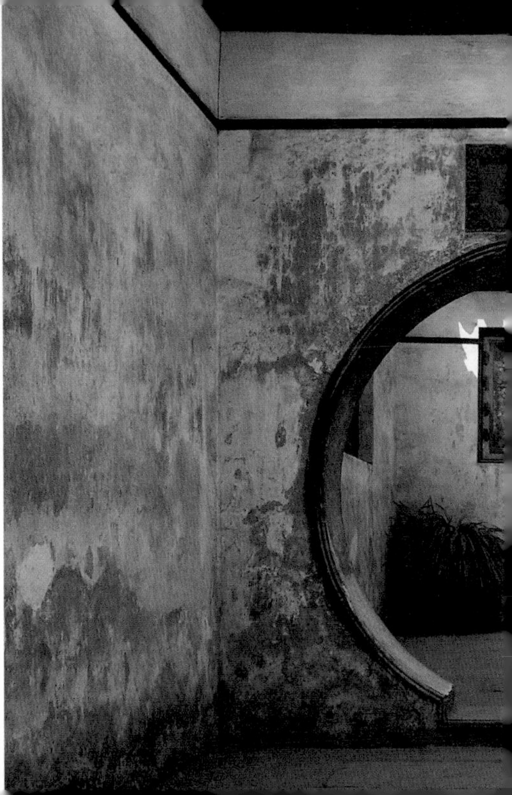

114 Shanghai, Yu yuan middle zone with 'river' and contorted rocks.

The most desirable rocks, celebrated for their rough, craggy and pock-marked form (*zhou, shou, tou*), came from Lake Tai (near Wuxi).

and subdivide it into 'rooms'; pavilions, varied in plan and shape, and open to the environment, are scattered apparently at random to frame and enjoy views and to provide space for living, sleeping, contemplation and study. Linked by verandahs and open galleries, circular moon-gates and doors of every conceivable shape lead from one zone to the next. Equally varied windows, usually screened with patterned lattices, frame 'living pictures' and provide visual links between zones not immediately accessible from one another. Axial routes are rejected in favour of zig-zag galleries, paths and bridges to recreate the impression of wandering freely in nature.

Nature provides the content. Stimulating rivers, real or contrived, run through the zones to feed reflective pools or lakes, again real or artificial, surrounded by real or artificial hills and chasms, and dotted with real or artificial islands, which invariably form the nucleus.[115] Around them both planting and building provide a succession of incidents awaiting discovery in circulation, a wilfully confusing variety which defeats any sense of command of the whole. Trees are stunted to conform to the scale of smaller gardens, and rocks of contorted shapes stand for the crags of famous

115 **Suzhou, Liu yuan (Garden for Lingering)** early 16th
century and restored in the early 19th century, view east
over the lake.

116 **Suzhou, Liu yuan** collection of miniature mountain
peaks and stunted trees.

117 **Wuxi, Jichang yuan** view to the south-east with a 'borrowed view' of the Longguang (Dragon Brilliance) pagoda.

beauty spots.[116] They also stand as witness to the force of nature and that collecting ever more bizarre examples was a cult. The uncontrollable is recalled also by the distant view of an eminence beyond the garden's confines – though often crowned with a pagoda.[117]

Of the many superb private retreats surviving in and around the cities of the south, cultivated by the Song, revived by the Ming and restored under the Qing, the intimate Wangshi yuan, the intense Liu yuan and the expansive Zhuozheng in Suzhou, the Yu yuan at Shanghai and the Jichang yuan in Wuxi are among the most celebrated gardens in China. The Qianlong emperor visited several of them and so particularly admired the Jichang yuan that he had its

118 OVERLEAF **Beijing, Yihe yuan** Wanshou shan (Ten-thousand Longevities Hill, right) and Kunming hu (Vast Bright Lake) with Zhihuihai si (Sea of Wisdom Temple, c. 1750, top right), Foxiang ge (Pagoda of the Buddha's Fragrance, late 19th-century replacement of a smaller, mid-18th-century structure, centre), the stele of the Qianlong emperor (1751) rising from the rebuilt court of the Zhuanlun cang (sutra library, lower right) and, rising from the edge of the lake, the roofs of the main palatine

temple, Paiyun dian (Hall that Dispels Clouds, with court and gate, left).

Incorporating the gardens of the Kangxi (1662–1722) and Yongzheng (1723–35) emperors, the Yuan Ming in the eastern part of the site was most celebrated in the accounts of 18th-century European travellers. Endowed by Jesuits in the service of the emperor with a grotesque palace in an Italianate rococo style, it was destroyed by British and French troops sent to Beijing to force concessions from the emperor in 1860. Splendidly integrated with its natural setting in the western sector of the site, the Yihe yuan was developed c. 1750 for the Qianlong emperor on the northern bank of an expanded lake (hence Kunming), and the south-facing slopes of a hill renamed in honour of the 60th birthday of the emperor's mother (hence Wanshou). Also largely destroyed in 1860, most of it was rebuilt in 1888, to celebrate the 60th birthday of the Dowager Empress Cixi, and again from 1902. For much of the 20 years before her death in 1908, Cixi ruled China from the palace at the north-east corner of the lake centred on Renshou dian (Hall of Happiness in Longevity).

119 **Beijing, Yihe yuan, Xiequ yuan** 1751, renovated
1811, view to the south-east.

views painted and reproduced as the Xiequ yuan (Garden of Harmonious Pleasure) of the Summer Palace at Beijing.[118-119]

Summer retreats

The Ming emperors developed summer retreats around the three lakes in the Imperial City, west of the Forbidden City, and they form the most popular parks of today's Beijing. The Qing emperors used them too, but resorted to the hills outside the Tartar city walls, to the north-west, and to Chengde in the mountains on the border of their Manchurian homeland (see 24, page 65). The Summer Palace on the outskirts of the capital, set in several gardens amalgamated by the Qianlong emperor, was largely destroyed by British and French troops in 1860 and subsequently rebuilt in part – though several 18th-century pavilions still command the view over the lake which originally recommended the site and the Xiequ yuan (see 118-119, pages 222-225) survives in embryo.

The fate of Chengde[120-124] has been somewhat happier. There the Kangxi emperor built a hunting lodge, and his grandson developed a garden paradise overlooked by an astonishing array of Lamaist monaster-

120 Chengde, Bishu shan zhuang (Mountain Village Where You Can Escape the Heat) 1703–c. 1780, interior.

Avoiding ostentation as a matter of policy, and frugal by nature, the Kangxi emperor made do with a miniature version of the Forbidden City incorporating nine courtyards and the six pavilions of the outer and inner zones. Like the others, the main hall, Danbojingcheng dian (Hall of Serene Frugality), is of unpainted cedar (whose fragrance, therefore, is unmasked) and is roofed with unglazed blue–grey tiles. The Qianlong emperor added a parallel range for his mother.

121 Chengde park, Shangdi lou (Tower of God Pagoda).

Beyond the northern gates of the palace compounds is a complex of warm lakes fed by a stream sourced from hot springs – making the site viable for much of the year. Beyond the lakes is the vast park – 5.5 square kilometres (2 square miles) enclosed by a wall 10 kilometres (6 miles) long. Both the Kangxi emperor and his grandson designated sets of 36 vantage points in the park, but neglected after the Jiaqing emperor died there in 1820, few survive. Of these the most notable are Shangdi lou (built on an artificial hill devised to recall the Jin Shan si on the Yangtze) and the Shui Xin xie (Three Pavilions in the Heart of the Water).

Some 11 temples were built between 1713 and 1780 on the hills surrounding the imperial park for visiting tribal chiefs or dignitaries from Tibet. Aligned on axes radiating from the palace, eight survive.

122 Chengde, Puning si (Temple of Universal Peace)
1755.

In variance of the Chinese tradition, Puning si was
supposedly built in homage to the most venerable of all
Tibetan temples, the Samye (see 17, page 53). It is nevertheless
axial in the Chinese tradition: gatehouse, court with bell and
drum towers, the court and Hall of the Heavenly King, and
the court and Hall of the Great Hero succeed one another in
the usual way, and even the climax is not without precedent.
This is the Dacheng ge, on a platform behind the Daoxiong
baodian that rises to 39 metres (130 feet) over a 28-metre
(90-foot) high statue of Guanyin. Apart from the numerous
bulbous dagobas on the terraces and crowning roof-ridges,
however, uncharacteristic of China are the heavy walls with
relatively small windows that mask traditional trabeation,
at least at the lower levels, and the multiple pyramidal roofs
with relatively large finials of the upper levels.

123 Chengde, Pule si (Temple of Universal Joy) 1766.

Like the earliest temples in the Chengde group – Puren si (Temple of Universal Love, 1713) in particular – and several later ones, Pule si conforms largely to Chinese tradition, though it was built to serve the devotions of the Mongol tribes who came annually to pay homage to the emperor. The Buddhism derived by the Mongols from the Tibetans was Tantric: in the double-roofed main pavilion, clearly inspired by the Qinian dian of the Tian tan in Beijing (see 84, page 165), the cruciform colonnade is a three-dimensional Tantric mandala, a circular cosmic diagram for guiding meditation.

ies dedicated to accommodating the tribal chiefs with whom he sought to maintain close contact. And from the surrounding peaks, transcending contrived enclosure as Chinese gardeners always do in borrowing the external view, the son of heaven naturally planned to embrace the world at large. That was his realm, cultivated under the mandate of heaven in perpetual harmony with *qi*. It transcends the terrestrial in effecting its perpetual concordance with *qi*'s cosmic currents, and never were the diviners of *feng shui* called to more spectacular account.

124 OVERLEAF Chengde, Xumifushou miao (Temple of Happiness and Longevity), Mount Sumeru c. 1780.

In homage to the Tibetan tradition, the temple was built to receive the Panchen Lama on his visit to Qianlong in 1780 under the inspiration of the Panchen's Tashilumpo monastery at Xigaze. The dominant element is a Chinese pavilion encased by a wall, and the whole is formidable only in appearance. Its axis crosses that of the sun rising between the *yang* and *yin* of the extraordinary phallic and mammalian features that dominate the spectacular site. Never have the dictates of *feng shui* been more felicitous.

glossary

ACROTERIA ornamental FINIALS, usually supported on a PLINTH, at the apex or side of a PEDIMENT.

AMBULATORY semicircular or polygonal arcade or walkway.

ANG diagonal cantilevered BEAM. (See page 104.)

APSE semicircular domed or vaulted space, especially at one end of a temple. Hence apsidal.

ARCADE series of arches supported by COLUMNS, sometimes paired and covered forming a walkway.

ARCHITRAVE one of the three principal elements of an ENTABLATURE, positioned immediately above the CAPITAL of a COLUMN, and supporting the FRIEZE and CORNICE.

BEAM horizontal element in, for instance, a TRABEATED structure.

BODHISATTVA previous incarnation of the Buddha, a compassionate spirit.

BRACKET projecting structural element providing support.

CAI unit of measurement based on the width of a DUO. (See page 94.)

CANTILEVER projecting element supporting a BEAM or CORNICE, for example.

CAPITAL top part of a COLUMN, supporting the ENTABLATURE, wider than the body of the SHAFT, usually formed and decorated more or less elaborately.

CHAITYA shrine or other sacred place or object.

CHAITYA-GRIHA type of Buddhist shrine evolved from a meeting hall.

CHATTRAVALI tiers forming the CHATTRI on top of the mound of a STUPA.

CHATTRI an umbrella-shaped dome or pavilion, sometimes acting as a turret on the roof of a STUPA.

CHIWEI decorative FINIAL on the ridge of a roof.

COFFERING decoration of a ceiling or VAULT with sunken rectangular or other polygonal panels.

COLONNADE line of regularly spaced COLUMNS.

COLUMN vertical member, usually circular in cross-section, functionally structural or ornamental, or both, comprising a base, SHAFT and CAPITAL.

CORNICE projecting moulding forming the top part of an ENTABLATURE.

CRYPTOPORTICO underground passage, frequently beneath a PORTICO.

CUSP projection formed between two arcs, especially in stone tracery, hence CUSPED.

CYMA REVERSA wave-shaped moulding, the upper part concave and the lower convex.

DAGOBA Buddhist reliquary, usually in the shape of a dome.

DAO hidden power of nature, hence DAOIST.

DE Confucian ideal of virtue.

DIAN large hall with a ceremonial or religious function.

DUO block, usually timber, at the top of column and supporting upper elements. (See page 94.)

DUOGONG combination of DUO and GONG at top of column, supporting main beam. (See page 94.)

EAVES part of a roof that overhangs the outer face of a wall.

ENTABLATURE part of the façade immediately above the COLUMNS, usually composed of a supportive ARCHITRAVE, decorative FRIEZE and projecting CORNICE.

FENG SHUI harmonisation with nature, hence system of bringing a building into harmony.

FINIAL ornament at the top of a GABLE or roof, for example.

FRESCO painting done on wet plaster.

FRIEZE middle part of an ENTABLATURE, above the ARCHITRAVE and below the CORNICE, or more generally any horizontal strip decorated in RELIEF.

GABLE more or less triangular vertical area defined by the ends of the inclined planes of a PITCHED ROOF.

GALLERY upper storey projecting over the main (usually interior) space of a building.

GAZEBO open structure commanding a prospect, sited in a garden or on a roof.

GONG carved cantilevered cross beam, usually timber, on top of the DUO, and supporting main beam. (See page 94.)

GONG Daoist temple.

HINAYANA the lesser vehicle towards salvation in the Buddhist tradition (as opposed to MAHAYANA).

HIP angle formed at the meeting of two inclined planes on a hipped roof.

HYPOSTYLE HALL hall with a roof supported by numerous COLUMNS more or less evenly spaced across its area.

JIAN bays of standard size, together defining the main interior of a building.

KAO GONG JI ancient Chinese town-planning treatise.

LAMA Buddhist religious master or priest.

LAMASERY Buddhist monastery.

LI unit of measurement, roughly 500 metres (550 yards).

LI Confucian ritual.

LINTEL horizontal member over, for example, a window or doorway, or bridging the gap between two COLUMNS or PIERS.

LULI residential block or walled district of a town

MADRASA Islamic school or college buildings, generally associated with a MOSQUE.

MAHAYANA the great vehicle towards salvation in the Buddhist tradition (as opposed to HINAYANA).

MANDAPA hall or pillared pavilion.

MEZZANINE intermediate storey often between ground and first floors.

MINARET tower attached to a MOSQUE, from which muslims are called to prayer.

MOSAIC decoration formed by embedding small, coloured tiles or pieces of glass (tesserae) in cement.

MOSQUE muslim temple/complex: defining physical embodiment of muslim ideology.

NICHE recess in a wall, usually containing a statue, for example.

OGEE ARCH composed of two CYMA REVERSA mouldings meeting head to head at the apex.

PAGODA Buddhist temple in the shape of a tower, with progressively smaller storeys, each with an elaborate and ornamental projecting roof.

PARAPET low wall, usually for defensive purposes.

PAVILION lightly constructed building, often tent-like and set in a garden, for example.

PEDIMENT triangular area of wall, usually a gable, above an ENTABLATURE.

PEIFANG ceremonial arch embodying an entrance screen. (See page 114.)

PIER supporting pillar for a wall or roof, often of rectangular cross-section.

PLINTH rectangular base or base support of a COLUMN or wall.

PODIUM projecting base or platform on which a building sits.

PORTICO entrance to a building featuring a COLONNADE.

POST vertical element in, for instance, a TRABEATED structure.

PRADAKSHINA ambulatory in a Buddhist monastery.

PRASADA multi-storey structure: mansion, palace or temple.

PURLIN horizontal beam running the length of a roof, resting on the main RAFTERS and supporting the subsidiary rafters.

QI will of heaven, spirit of nature. (See page 11.)

RAFTER roof timber, usually sloping down from the ridge to the EAVES, and supporting the outer covering of the roof.

RAMPART defensive earthwork, usually surrounding a fortress or citadel, often with a stone PARAPET.

RELIEF raised carving, usually of figures, made by cutting away more (HIGH RELIEF) or less (LOW RELIEF) of the material from which they are carved.

REVETMENT reinforced, often decorative, facing for a wall.

ROOF, HIPPED roof composed of a PITCHED ROOF with inclined (as opposed to vertical) planes at the ends.

ROOF, PITCHED roof composed of two inclined planes whose point of contact forms the ridge or highest line.

SARCOPHAGUS outer coffin of stone, often highly decorated.

SHAFT more or less cylindrical element of a COLUMN rising from the base to the CAPITAL.

SHENG small block, usually timber, on top of a GONG, supporting a beam. (See page 94.)

SHIKHARA superstructure of a north Indian Hindu temple.

SI Buddhist temple.

STELE upright stone marker, often a tombstone, in the shape of a column or panel, usually with a decorative carving and/or inscription.

STRUT timber element, especially supporting a RAFTER.

STUCCO type of plaster, especially used where decoration is to be applied.

STUPA pre-eminent type of Buddhist monument, a tumulus, burial or reliquary mound.

SUTRA sacred Buddhist text.

TANTRISM Buddhist doctrine associated with a group of mystical works – the tantras.

TERRACOTTA baked clay used for construction or decoration of buildings or statues.

TESSELATED patterned surface composed of small blocks, such as MOSAIC.

TING reception hall or pavilion, usually open-sided and situated in a garden. (See page 207.)

TRABEATED structurally dependent on rectilinear POST and BEAM supports.

TUMULUS ancient burial mound.

VERANDAH roofed COLONNADE attached to one or more sides of a building.

VESTIBULE courtyard in front of the entrance to a house; hallway to a building; space adjunct to a larger room.

VIMANA storeyed building with receding terraces, used in southern India as the main element of a sanctuary.

WATTLE AND DAUB method of making walls using twigs (wattles) interwoven and then plastered with mud or clay (daub).

XIA summer-house or GAZEBO. (See page 207.)

XUAN summer-house or GAZEBO reserved as a retreat for study. (See page 207.)

YUAN garden or courtyard.

The books listed below are those the author found particularly useful as sources of general information on the architecture covered in this volume.

Liu, Laurence G, *Chinese Architecture,* London 1989
Sickman, L and Soper, A, *The Art and Architecture of China*, third edition, Harmondsworth 1968
Wu, Nelson I, *Chinese and Indian Architecture*, London and New York 1953
Historic Chinese Architecture, Beijing 1985

bibliography

index

Figures in bold refer to the text; those in ordinary type refer to captions; and those in ordinary type with an asterisk refer to illustrations.

This 25-volume series tells the story of architecture from the earliest settlements in the Euphrates and Jordan valleys to the sophisticated buildings of the late twentieth century. Each volume sets the buildings described and illustrated within their political, social, cultural and technological contexts, exploring architecture not only as the development of form but as an expression of the civilisations within which it evolved. The series focuses on the classical tradition from its origins, through its seminal realisation in ancient Greece and Rome, to the Renaissance, neo-classicism, eclecticism, modernism and post-modernism, supplemented with excursions to India and south-east Asia.

CHRISTOPHER TADGELL teaches architectural history at the Kent Institute of Art and Design and has lectured widely in Britain and the USA.

VOLUMES 1 TO 9

• • • **a history of architecture** christopher tadgell **9**

japan
the informal contained

The history of the people of the Japanese archipelago has been moulded by an idiosyncratic conservatism, admitting change, but supplementing rather than supplanting existing institutions. The same characteristics have shaped the architectural development described in this book, with foreign influences and forms, principally from China, absorbed and transformed.

The Japanese are masters of the assymetrical and the direct relationship between building and nature. The former can be seen in the contrast between the first imperial cities, laid out on a grid under the influence of Tang China, and the organic growth of towns in and around the precincts of castles as foreign influence receded. As ritual was elaborated, moreover, the native predilection for informality and studied simplicity achieved its full expression in both shrine and house.

Zen Buddhism, introduced in the 13th century, also lead to the development of garden design, not a literal reproduction of nature, but abstraction calculated to elicit a subjective response.